*Agape in the New Testament*

VOLUME I

CESLAUS SPICQ, O.P.

# AGAPE IN THE NEW TESTAMENT

*Volume One*

*Agape in the Synoptic Gospels*

TRANSLATED BY
Sister Marie Aquinas McNamara, O.P.
AND
Sister Mary Honoria Richter, O.P.

*Wipf & Stock*
PUBLISHERS
*Eugene, Oregon*

IMPRIMATUR ✠ Joseph Cardinal Ritter
Archbishop of St. Louis, September 13, 1963

Wipf and Stock Publishers
199 W 8th Ave, Suite 3
Eugene, OR 97401

Agape in the New Testament
Agape in the Synoptic Gospels
By Spicq, Ceslaus
Copyright©1963 Province Dominicaine de France
ISBN: 1-59752-856-0
Publication date 8/7/2006
Previously published by Herder Book Co., 1963

# Introduction

It has sometimes been said that, since everything our Lord did was a manifestation of love, to collect the biblical texts concerning charity would be to reproduce the entire New Testament. Each of its verses is a revelation of love, of *agape*. *Agape*, love of charity, is a central concept of the New Covenant; it is a reality common to God, to Christ, and to men. Its manifestations are so plentiful and various that the development of a New Testament theology deriving from charity is perfectly possible.

Before the synthesis can be constructed, however, it will be necessary to discover exactly what "love of charity" is. Modern studies have concentrated on its objects and acts, especially on the relation of love of neighbor to love of God, but they have not first defined its nature. Exactly what did our Lord Jesus Christ and his apostles understand by the word "charity"? In a previous work [C. Spicq, *Agapè, Prolégomènes à une Etude de théologie néo-testamentaire*, Louvain, 1955] we attempted to answer this question by studying the semantics of *agapan* (to love) in classical Greek and in the papyri. This study was concluded by an examination of rabbinical morality, which had tried to establish the relation between the fear of God and the love of God.

We now propose to determine the meaning of the word "charity" in the first century A.D. and to understand not only the morality taught by our Lord but also the whole

## Introduction

religion of love revealed and founded by him. Even at first reading, the New Testament texts show a new and decisive evolution, both semantic and doctrinal, of the verb *agapan* and its derivatives. Therefore an examination of each of the texts containing these words, as far as possible in chronological order, to determine the nuances of their meanings in context is important. This examination is the object of the present volume. The author has tried to discover the exact import of each verse through a series of exegetical analyses. Partial conclusions, drawn throughout the work, will show relationships which are fundamental to a theology of *agape*. The Christian religion established itself gradually—from Christ through St. James, St. Paul, and St. Peter to St. John—as a function of love. Between the Sermon on the Mount and the Apocalypse, "charity" evolved, the notion becoming richer and more precise while remaining homogeneous, since the apostles' teaching was an explanation of the charity revealed by Jesus. A study of the history of the word *agape* will reveal the evolution of the concept and make it possible to penetrate its profundity.

This volume is simply a presentation of materials ready for use in constructing a New Testament theology of charity. It has its own value, however, both as an exhaustive anthology of the texts in the New Revelation relative to *agape* and, much more, as the progressive clarification of the concept. Contemporary Christian thought, to its honor, has exalted charity's unrivaled value in the economy of salvation. Nevertheless, serious misunderstanding about the very quality of this love, its origin, or even its authentic manifestations still persist. It is too often forgotten that any biblical theology worthy of the

## Introduction

name depends intrinsically upon philological exegesis. Only notions that are expressed or implied in the vocabulary and in the language of the inspired authors can be attributed to them. Of course, those writers spoke in the name of God and transmitted his word, but they did it through their own human expressions, which the Holy Spirit personally assumed and guaranteed. No one has the right, therefore, to use the specifically Christian word "charity" in any sense different from the language of the New Testament. For example, A. Nygren, whose work is considered authoritative, is gravely mistaken about the New Testament meaning of *agape,* perhaps because his analysis has been vitiated by dogmatic prejudice or perhaps because he worked from too limited a choice of texts.

It has seemed to us indispensable, therefore, both for the sake of sound methodology and because of the seriousness of the undertaking, to make a minute and objective analysis of each use of *agapan, agape, agapetos* —to love, love, beloved. We have been particularly careful to note the Hellenistic parallels wherever possible, especially those of the papyri, the contemporary popular language. Finally, we have taken the interpretations of the best ancient and modern exegetes into account. We have every hope of understanding what our Lord and his apostles meant when they spoke of "love" of God, "love" for God, and "love" for men.

C.S.

# Translators' Preface

Father Spicq's beautiful and important work on *agape* has been inaccessible to anyone who does not read French, yet it is one of the most valuable works for the study of charity, the unique virtue, as it is set forth in the New Testament. Its conclusions are of central importance to an understanding of what it is to be a Christian. The Christian's thoughts and actions flow from his being, which is the very being of Christ, of God, who is love. Father Spicq's work examines all the New Testament texts concerning love, *agape*. These texts reveal that the life of the Trinity, God's relations with men and men's with him, and men's relations with one another are all functions of the one love that is God's own nature. The Christian behaves according to what he is, a person whose being arises from freely-given love, from *agape*. Thus the book has extraordinary value in unifying and deepening the reader's sense of who he is and of what he must do. Any materialistic conception of the spiritual life as a perfection pursued by whittling off a trait here and adding another there, to the eventual construction of a flawless performer is shown to be inaccurate. "Be ye perfect as your heavenly Father is perfect." The perfection of love does give rise to the flawless performance Scripture demands, but perfection is not constructed from flawless performances. Performance flows from love, and love is the perfect gift of the loving God.

*Agapè dans le Nouveau Testament* is a scholarly work,

*Translators' Preface*

but an appreciation of its treasures in no way depends on an appreciation of the intricacies of Father Spicq's techniques of investigation. The ease and apparent simplicity with which idea after idea is added to the first notion of charity, enriching it without altering it, make the book valuable and moving for everyone. It resembles the Scripture on which it is based in being both sublime and matter of fact: "This is my well-beloved son. . ."; "Charity is kind, is patient." The three thick volumes of the French edition of *Agapè* contain nearly as many words of technical footnotes as they do of text. The notes are indispensable to the professional exegete or philologist, but to the general reader for whom this translation is intended, they would be of very little interest. We have omitted most of the footnotes, therefore, and retained only a nontechnical few. The text itself of the first volume has not been altered or shortened except for the omission of two appendices. The original bibliography of works in French, German, English, Italian, Dutch, Spanish, and Latin has been omitted also, since those who would find it useful will undoubtedly prefer to consult the work in the original.

It has seemed better to alter the French method of division into volumes. The original comprises three volumes of uniform size, but none contains a "unit" of study. The English version will have three volumes of unequal size, but each volume will be complete in itself. The first contains all the analyses of the synoptic Gospels; the second, of the Acts and epistles except those of St. John; and the third of St. John's epistles, his Gospel, and the Apocalypse.

All Greek expressions except *agapan* (to love) and its

*Translators' Preface*

derivatives have been rendered in English. The Kleist and Lilly translation of the New Testament and the Confraternity translation of the Old Testament have been used, for the most part, for scriptural quotations.

# Contents

Introduction, v

Translators' Preface, ix

## Chapter I: Agape in the Gospel of St. Matthew

The Verb *Agapan*, 5

*Divine and fraternal charity*, 8
*Charity, exclusive choice and service of God*, 16
*Love of neighbor, moral precept and spiritual perfection*, 19
*Charity toward God and neighbor, foundation and inspiration of morality in the kingdom of heaven*, 26

The Noun *Agape*, 32

*The growing cold of charity through tribulation*, 32

The Adjective *Agapetos*, 36

*The divine proclamation at Christ's baptism*, 37
*The divine proclamation at the transfiguration*, 41
*The authentic character of the Messias*, 46

Conclusion, 49

*God's love for his son*, 49
*The love of men for God*, 51
*The love of Christians for other men*, 52
*The degrees and death of charity*, 54
*The morality of love*, 55

## Chapter II: Agape in the Gospel of St. Mark

The Verb *Agapan*, 59

*The love of Jesus for the rich young man,* 59
*The greatest commandment is to love,* 62

    The Adjective *Agapetos,* 67

*Jesus, beloved of his Father,* 67

    Conclusion, 72

*God loves his son and other men,* 72
*Jesus loves other men,* 73
*Christian charity,* 73

## Chapter III: Agape in the Gospel of St. Luke

    The Verb *Agapan,* 77

*Fraternal charity,* 77
*The centurion's esteem for the Jewish nation,* 92
*The charity of the sinful woman,* 95
*Charity prescribed for the Scribe and accomplished by the Samaritan,* 108
*Love of applause and of being first,* 118
*Charity, exclusive choice and service of God,* 120

    The Noun *Agape,* 120

*The primacy of charity toward God,* 120

    The Adjective *Agapetos,* 122

    Conclusion, 122

## Chapter IV: Conclusion: Agape in the Synoptic Gospels, 127

    List of Texts Analyzed, 145

    Index, 146

## Agape in the Synoptic Gospels

*The number of times the verb* agapan *(to love) and its derivatives appear in the New Testament suggests something of the importance and evolution of the specifically Christian doctrine of charity. The New Testament texts contain the verb* agapan *(to love) 141 times; the noun* agape *(love) 117 times; the adjective* agapetos *(beloved) 61 times.*

Agapan *is used 25 times in the synoptic Gospels,* agape *only twice (not at all in St. Mark), and* agapetos *eight times (three times in St. Matthew, three times in St. Mark, and twice in St. Luke).*

# CHAPTER I

# Agape in the Gospel of St. Matthew

## The verb *agapan*

THE verb *agapan* occurs eight times in St. Matthew's Gospel and each time our Lord himself uses it. Four of its five appearances in the Sermon on the Mount are in the imperative mood (Mt. 5:43, 44, 46 [twice]; 6:24). The first Gospel is of special importance in determining the meaning of charity, not only because it is the oldest of the New Testament texts, but also and particularly because charity is commanded in the Sermon on the Mount, which is the very charter of the kingdom founded by Christ.

Christ's tone of authority as he solemnly directs and commands is striking. He is obviously speaking as the new Moses, but with the authority (Mt. 7:29) of the Messias sent by God (Mt. 5:17; Mk. 1:38), who had come at last to establish a new economy of salvation: "I, on the contrary, declare to you." He is legislator, enacting the constitution of his kingdom, and promulgator, setting forth the New Law. The statements that follow are like paragraphs of a code, succeeding one another without apparent relation or connection.

The Sermon was intended to establish the superiority of the New Law over the Old. "Do not think it is my mission to annul the Law or the Prophets. It is not my mission to annul, but to bring to perfection. . . . Yes, let me tell you: if your religion is not very much better than that of the Scribes and Pharisees, you will never enter the kingdom of heaven" (Mt. 5:17–20). Our Lord intended in this sermon to persuade as well as to explain.

## Agape in the New Testament

He declared that he would not make a sharp break with the past by annulling the moral law prescribed by the Old Testament; that law remained an expression of the divine will. He, however, its authorized interpreter, would "fulfill and complete" the old economy. His disciples must possess a justice of a higher order than the justice of contemporary Judaism.

By substituting "Scribes and Pharisees" for "the Law or the Prophets," Christ showed that he was speaking of the official Jewish interpretation of the precepts of the Old Covenant and not of their literal meanings. It was not the old legislation itself that he modified—it contained the seed of his own teaching—but the way it was understood and practiced. Christ did not come to construct a system of morality, with principles, statements, balances, nuances, and concrete applications; he came to bring men into the kingdom of heaven. His listeners all hoped to arrive at the kingdom. Because the Scribes and Pharisees possessed true "justice," they felt sure of access, but Jesus declared their justice insufficient and demanded a higher justice of his disciples. The question was not one of more of the same kind of righteousness, but of better justice, a new justice, different in its very nature. Christ revealed the true spiritual meaning of the Law: the law is to love.

Such a revelation was necessary because the Judaism of Christ's time had, in practice, identified morality with legalism. It did indeed conceive the life of the just person, or better the pious person, as religious, that is, as obedient to the All-Powerful God. Virtue was simply the strict observance of the Law, the expression of the divine will. Judaism had come to the point of hypostatizing the Law, as it were, in considering it independent of God himself. Thus its fundamental meaning had been blurred. The living Word had been divided into a multitude of precepts, commandments, prohibitions, interdictions, each with its independent value, so that the *cult of the letter* (2 Cor. 3:6) had become a truly insupportable yoke (Acts 15:10). Each observance of each point, *iota*, of the Law earned a reward. Each action in conformity with the rule was a good action and merited a return. The ideal was to accumulate good works in a sort of treasure hoard. The "just man" kept an account with God, so to speak, and considered himself a creditor dealing with his debtor.

Christ opposed a true morality characterized by interiority to this legalism of purely material fidelity to the commandments; the observance of the letter gave way to the promptings of the Spirit. What counts for entrance into the kingdom of heaven is interior justice, disposition of the soul, and, above all, the gift of self to God. Purity of heart is essential, not exterior acts. Evidently this interiority singularly simplifies and unifies the moral life. The uninstructed, simple people who could never unravel the tangled precepts of the complicated code, could, nevertheless, adhere to God and prove their fidelity to him. Even sinners were called to the kingdom if they would open their hearts to the divine initiative. God loves the man, not his works.

The new morality of the Sermon on the Mount depends upon a new concept of God. No longer a stern banker handing down statements of profit and loss according to an exact balance sheet, he is now a Father—a loving Father. The members of his kingdom are no longer the just or the faithful; they are now his dear children. Children imitate their fathers; hence the morality of the members of the kingdom is a filial morality. They make a loving gift of their hearts to their father and confidently abandon themselves to his kindness and providence. The New Testament teaching on charity must be understood in terms of this fundamental revelation. This teaching eminently displays both the transcendence and the fidelity of the New Law in relation to the Old. The essential spirit of the Messianic kingdom is visible in charity.

#### DIVINE AND FRATERNAL CHARITY

You have heard it said: "*Love your neighbor* and hate your enemy." I, on the contrary, declare to you: *love your enemies* and pray for your persecutors, and thus prove yourselves children of your Father in heaven. He, certainly, lets his sun rise upon bad and good alike, and makes the rain fall on sinners as well as saints. Really, *if you love those that love you*, what reward do you deserve? Do not tax collectors do as much? And if you have a friendly greeting for your brothers only, are you doing anything out of the common? Do not the heathen do as much? Be perfect, then, as your heavenly Father is perfect (Mt. 5:43–48).

The text does not define charity, but rather describes it in its acts and motives. Composed in the favorite Israelite idiom of a succession of antitheses, it presents the points of view of legislative or of traditional authority first: "You have heard it said." The impersonal form obscures the source, Leviticus 19:18, of the ancient precept, quoted here in part by Christ. Moses had prescribed:

## Agape in the Gospel of St. Matthew

"You will love your neighbor *as yourself.*" "Neighbor" meant companion or compatriot. A foreigner who had been absorbed into the Israelite community, a proselyte "who had come over," was "neighbor" too. He could be loved "as oneself" because "no one can hate his own flesh" (Eph. 5:29).

Although the Old Testament certainly never prescribed hatred of enemies, it did command an anathema against the Moabites, the Ammonites, the Amalecites, and others. No one was to pardon them or to make an alliance with them. Foreigners might be lawfully oppressed (Dt. 7:2; 15:3; 20:13–18; 23:4–7; 25:17–19). The principle of conduct was to return whatever kind of treatment another had offered (Ps. 137:8; Mt. 5:38), since that was the way Yahweh himself behaved toward his enemies (Mal. 1:2–5). Since the Hebrew language contained no words for expressing any feelings between those of love and hate, the Old Law's prescribing charity for a strictly limited circle of compatriots did, in a sense, condone hatred of enemies. To love an enemy was an offense against common sense as well as against decent self-interest. The people were indignant when the king was grieving over his son Absalom's death. Joab reproached him: "Thou hast shamed this day the faces of all thy servants, that have saved thy life and the lives of thy sons and of thy daughters and the lives of thy wives and the lives of thy concubines. Thou lovest them that hate thee, and thou hatest them that love thee" (2 Sm. 19:5–6). This typically Semitic text opposes love and hate under the form of predilection accorded to one and refused to another, or preference for one over another. The precept in Leviticus to love one's neighbor

## Agape in the New Testament

was probably glossed by a mention of its opposite, hatred of enemies. The associated ideas, love of neighbor-hatred of enemies, may have been expressed in a popular saying of the first century, "Love your neighbor, and hate your enemy," referred to by our Lord (Mt. 5:43). An equivalent form has recently been found in the *Manual of Discipline* discovered at Qumran.

Christ made his opposition to this current concept of morality very plain. He did more than suggest a change; he commanded, in virtue of his own authority: "I, on the contrary, declare to you." He repeated the Mosaic commandment of fraternal love (Mt. 19:19), but annulled what tradition had taken to be its limits by the formulation of his own extremely significant precept. We might gloss: "With regard to love, you must love everyone, even your enemies." Jesus opposed exegesis to exegesis. First he quoted the divine precept of love of neighbor and cited its current interpretation as excluding enemies. He then announced on his own authority the true meaning of this permanent commandment as it would be observed in his kingdom from then on: Love both your neighbor and your enemy! There is no need of microscopic lexicographic or exegetical analyses to determine what this new object of charity is or how "enemy" is opposed to "neighbor." St. Matthew's text furnishes an abundance of perfectly clear synonyms.

"Neighbor" (v. 43) is the same as "the good" and "the saints" (v. 45), "those who love us" (v. 46), and "brothers" (v. 47). "Enemies" (vv. 43–44) are "your persecutors" (v. 44), "the bad," and "sinners" (v. 45). Thus the context shows that Christ did not envisage "enemy" primarily in a national or political sense, as the word might be understood today to mean any man separated from another by a frontier, a language, or opposing interests. Our Lord's precept was far more "interior." It was concerned with disposition of soul, and thus preserved exactly the spirit of Leviticus which it fulfilled. It asks us not to take personal antipathies or feelings of bitterness or animosity into account (cf. vv. 39–44). We must love our neighbor—good or bad, fair or unfair, kind or difficult; neither race, religion, nor nationality make any difference.

Does this mean that we must love to the same degree and in the same way both those who have been good to us and those who have been hostile? No. For one thing, St. Matthew is using the verb *agapan* for "love," not the verb *philein*, "to love in friendship." It is impossible to have friendship with an enemy; *philia* implies a reciprocal love, an exchange, even a common life. Some kind of warm feeling for a sinner or for an unpleasant person is not demanded, at least not expressly. Primarily, *agapan* means to show respect and kindness. Even to enemies we owe esteem, fair treatment, and help in time of need. We truly show love toward them, because we wish them good things and do everything possible to see that they get them. Besides, Jesus himself explained the precept: "You must love your enemies with charity," by adding, "Pray for those who persecute you." Just as "your persecutors" is synonymous with "your enemies," the verb "to pray for" corresponds with "to love." To ask God for some favor which our persecutor will not let us provide for him is an undeniable sign of our sincere wish to do him good. We do not cling to our own judgment concerning the rights and wrongs of the disagreement that separates us. We invoke God and rise above the sphere of human relations, in order to further our enemy's true good. Prayer is the greatest and most far-reaching kindness, *agape*'s most expressive and always possible proof.

The examples our Lord gives show that *agape* is not a sentimental feeling, but the intention of doing good; it is not a hidden affection, but a profound desire searching for means of expression. Unlike the pagans, who greet and show consideration only to their brothers, we imitate God, who never tires of giving his gifts to all men without distinction.

Christ's disciples can be recognized by the way they practice fraternal charity. Publicans and heathens love only their neighbors and those who love them. This kind of love is good and to be approved, not abolished, but it is so natural and spontaneous that it does not deserve any special praise or reward. Our Lord prescribes something more for his disciples (cf. 6:7): not only that they love their enemies but also that they imitate God himself. This transcendent motive is the justification for the universal extension of charity. When we limit our affection to our brothers or to our neighbors, we can love them "as ourselves" because our love for them is an extension of our love for ourselves; it is the same kind of love we have for ourselves. When it becomes necessary to love those who are disagreeable or even dangerous, we can desire their good and love them truly only if we have a higher inspiration: "in order to be sons of our Father who is in heaven." No doubt, this motive clothes even our enemies with a true lovableness, but the accent of the pericope is on their *need* for help, a need we have no right to ignore and to leave unanswered.

## Agape in the Gospel of St. Matthew

The point of the argument is in the relation of father to son; a child is like his father, not only in physical appearance, but also in nature, outlook, and behavior. Christ's disciples are called to aspire to this divine sonship, and St. John tells us that adhering to Christ really does establish them in this divine relationship (Jn. 1:12). Thereafter it is a matter of being faithful to the newly-received nature and to its spirit. We must conduct ourselves, not like "illegitimate children," according to the strong expression of Hebrews 12:8, but in a manner worthy of true sons. Since the broadest, most efficacious fraternal charity is the sign of divine filiation, it implies that God is love, and therefore good and generous. The Old Testament, especially the Psalms, had sung the benignity of Yahweh and his generous kindness. When Moses asked God to let him see his glory, that is, his nature, Yahweh answered in equivalent terms: "I will make all my beauty pass before you" (Ex. 33:18–19), and explained that he granted grace and mercy. In performing his acts of kindness he makes absolutely no distinction between the good and the perverse; he favors one as much as the other. God's sons, then, will practice the *same* kindness: they pray to their Father for their enemies; they do not hesitate to love the unloving; they show affection for those who ignore their kindnesses or who do them harm.

The conclusion is extraordinary: "Be perfect, then, as your heavenly Father is perfect." Although the Old Testament required the Israelites to be holy (Lv. 11:44–45; 19:2) and perfect before God (Dt. 18:13) because he himself is holy, these prescriptions were entirely negative; they cautioned men to avoid sin. Not one text conceived of charity under its most generous form of love of enemies, much less as the love proper to sons who show that they have in their own hearts the charity of their Father in heaven. Charity's extension to all, demanded of men because exemplified in God, implies a unique and deeply mysterious quality in the Christian, as St. John and St. Paul later made clear. Christians are distinguished from pagans and from publicans by more than their belonging to the Lord whose orders they execute and whose spirit they imitate. Their relation with God goes beyond the moral order of obedience and fidelity and even beyond the order of religious consecration envisaged in the Pentateuch; the relation, we would say today, is of a divine order.

In other words, to love both neighbor and enemy as God loves them, they must actually be sons of God in the strictest sense of the word. Only those who have God for their Father share his love and are able to do what he does—include all men in his charity. The fullness of love in the disciple's heart displays itself in love's universal extension. Whoever loves universally is perfect because he does what is prescribed in verse 45: "Therefore prove yourselves children of your Father in heaven."

When Jesus affirmed: "I, on the contrary, declare to you: love your enemies," it was clear that he spoke of perfect charity. The comparison with the affection pagans have for one another—"do not they do as much?"—implies that Christian love exceeds the common measure—"are you doing anything out of the common?" In giving them God as an example, Christ passes to a superior order; only God and his children know how to envelop all men in their love. The last precept in verse 48 repeats verse 44 by identifying fraternal charity with perfection. To love even enemies is to be perfect, but much more, it is to be perfect with the very perfection of God: "Be perfect, therefore, as your heavenly Father is perfect." The repetition of the word "perfect" accentuates the union of men with God, of children with their Father, through love.

The elevated tone of the first canonical Gospel should not be surprising. St. Matthew presents another equally profound and authentic insight in the logion of the revelation of the Father and the Son (Mt. 11:25–27), where a Johannine tone is generally recognized. When he defined his kingdom's charter on the Mount, Christ revealed everything he would entrust to his apostles to explain and to develop. The Lord sowed the seed; God, who is love, is the Father; men united to him by faith are his children; their works manifest that they share his nature —love. A good tree cannot bear bad fruit. By his fruits of charity the Christian knows himself to be the Lord's disciple.

Long meditation on the whole Sermon on the Mount makes it clear that Christ is not prescribing particular attitudes or specifying exactly what is to be done to imitate or to obey God. The actions he describes are examples, given in a paradoxical form that could not be literally accomplished. What he requires is a new and permanent disposition of soul; this disposition is the essence of his morality. He had defined it negatively as a justice superior to that of the Scribes and of Pharisees. Verse 48 formulates it positively as an interior perfection of the same completely spiritual nature as God's perfection.

The verse summarizes all the teaching, beginning from verse 21, but puts the emphasis on fraternal charity. To become part of the kingdom of God just being founded, it was not enough to be virtuous in the philosophic sense nor to be obedient to the commandments as prescribed by Judaism; it was necessary to become the child of God. Only this community of nature and of life could make it possible to love as God loves. In his first great sermon, our Lord insisted particularly upon the "extraordinary" manifestations of this love. Later, his apostles emphasized the divine sonship such love implies. "Beloved, let us love one another, because love takes its origin in God, and everyone that loves is a child of God and knows God" (1 Jn. 4:7).

CHARITY, EXCLUSIVE CHOICE AND SERVICE OF GOD

A man cannot be the slave of two masters. He will either hate the one and *love* the other, or at least, be attentive to the one and neglectful of the other. You cannot have money and God for masters (Mt. 6:24).

Our Lord had just forbidden the amassing of perishable riches, always likely to be lost in this world. He instructed his followers to accumulate "goods" that would be secure in heaven—in modern terminology we would say "capital." They could lay up this "treasure" by doing good works and especially by being faithful to the Beatitudes (5:3–12). They must learn wisdom. Our Lord was not prescribing right use of this world's goods nor poverty of spirit nor almsgiving, but rather attachment of soul to true spiritual goods. An attachment of this kind implies a detachment from the world's riches, as

## Agape in the Gospel of St. Matthew

Christ said forcefully in verse 21: "After all, where your treasure is, there, too, your heart is bound to be." Man binds himself to what is good for him, to *his* good. He will put his whole heart into trying to acquire whichever is more precious to him, spiritual or material riches, and will pay no attention to the other.

This fundamental choice is expressed by the verb *agapan* in verse 24. No alternative is possible; man will serve God or he will serve his own desires. He must choose one of two masters, each of whom has such a hold on his slaves that he controls them completely, leaving them no possibility of doing any work but his own or giving any time to another master. More accurately, however, the servant chooses his master, like an investor who chooses the enterprise that will give him the best profit for his money. The disciple is warned against trying to give part of his devotion to each of these two all-demanding masters. Jesus declared categorically that plurality is absolutely impossible: "No one can be the slave . . . of two. . . . You cannot have both for masters. . . ."

A choice must be made, and choice involves sacrifice. St. Matthew and St. Luke preserve here the significance *agapan* had in Deuteronomy: to choose and to prefer.[1] Its association, as in this text, with the idea of serving is frequent and adds the notion of loving jealously or even of adoring to the idea of choice and preference. Our text is obviously concerned with religious love and with

---

[1] Because the substitution of *philein* for *agapan* would make this text unintelligible, the verse is one of the strongest in the Bible in favor of the distinction between the two verbs. *Philia*, no matter what its preferences, is not exclusive and admits several persons at one time to participation in friendship.

exclusive attachment. To adore God—King of kings and Lord of lords—necessitates belonging to him body and soul and serving him to the exclusion of other masters.

The point of the text is in this fundamental religious choice, expressed in a "two-part rhythm" frequently found in St. Matthew. The synonym used for *agapan* is *antechesthai*—to be attentive to—a verb of duration and of fidelity, implying permanence in its attachment. It means "to cling to" (Ti. 1:9), often with the idea of resisting difficulties or opposition (1 Thes. 5:14). Used with the genitive of person, as it is here, the verb means "not to tire in taking care of, to dedicate oneself to an austere task"; it also retains here the meaning it has in the Septuagint: "to give honor to God or idols, to extol them."

The opposite of "to love" is expressed not only by its obvious antonym, "to hate," but also by the verb "to be neglectful of" (*kataphronein*), exactly as it was understood in the Septuagint and in the best classical Greek: "to despise, disdain, set no value on, refuse to consider or to interest oneself." Where God is concerned, disdain is vile outrage.

Thus the text again applies the verb pair "to love" and "to hate" already used of love of neighbor, but this time it applies them to love of God. Moreover, it shows that *agapan* implies, just as in classical Greek, a judgment of esteem that inspires homage, devotion, and fidelity. As in the Septuagint, *agapan* is a verb of religious love and adoration expressing undivided consecration to God and to his service. Jesus asks his disciples to give their whole hearts to the one true God—according to the formula of the first commandment—explaining that their giving must be so definitive and complete that they become like slaves bound to him body and soul. No other attraction will have any interest for them; no extraneous force can hold dominion in their souls. To allow themselves to be invaded by any other influence and to be divided would be to betray the one true God.

LOVE OF NEIGHBOR, MORAL PRECEPT
AND SPIRITUAL PERFECTION

And *love* your neighbor as yourself (Mt. 19:19).

The text is the full quotation of Leviticus 19:18, which was given only in part in Matthew 5:43. Our Lord had just left Galilee to go into Perea. An unknown man came up to him and asked, "Rabbi, is there something good that I can do so as to win eternal life?" Our Lord answered: "Why do you consult me about something good you could do? There is One who is absolutely good! If you want to enter eternal life, keep the commandments." "Which?" the man asked. And Jesus said: "These: 'Do not murder; do not commit adultery; do not steal; do not bear false witness; honor father and mother; and, love your neighbor as yourself.' " "I have observed all these things," the young man replied, "What am I still lacking?" "If you want to be perfect," Jesus said to him, "go and sell all your possessions and give the proceeds to the poor—for which you will have an investment in heaven; then come back and be my follower." When the young man heard the answer, he went away with a heavy heart; for "he had much property."

The rich young man was a product of the most orthodox Judaism. His soul was beautifully sensitive to religious values and enamored of moral perfection. Moved by Christ's preaching and influence, he had come to consult the master about the basic problem of all spiritual life: how to obtain eternal life. The way he put his question, however, revealed a spirituality typical of the Pharisees. What works must I perform to be sure of obtaining the supreme reward? It seems that he wanted a sort of guarantee, "insurance" for the future, as it were. He took eternal life for an acquisition which ought to be registered in due form as soon as he accomplished whatever good things would elicit God's pleasure and his reward. Perhaps he thought the new master would know the procedure for securing this life.

Our Lord's answer was intended to rid the young man subtly of his juridical and entirely too material idea of the moral and religious life. When eternal life is in question, "works" are not so much what count as the very person of God, who grants life as a gift. All the "good" that men can do has only relative value (Is. 64:5) and can never constitute a strict right to the good that is properly divine. Jesus suggested, therefore, the futility of inquiries on the juridico-moral level; "Why do you consult me about something good you could do? There is One who is absolutely good." For the neuter "something good"—implying a commandment to be obeyed—he substituted a masculine "One"; for preoccupation with things, he substituted God in person.

The young man's intention, however, was straightforward, and our Lord responded to the deep yearning he recognized in him. With the authority of a divinely accredited prophet he told him that the Mosaic commandments, the expression of God's will, were the means of entering eternal life. This information might have been enlightening to a proselyte, but to the young man it appeared entirely too elementary. He already had considerably more than a beginner's knowledge of religion and wanted to rise above the level of moral correctness. His interest lay in theological problems; he seems even to have had a lucid experience of the spiritual life. Taking Christ's answer seriously, he supposed these "commandments" to be some special precepts reserved for the perfect. His "which?" was a request to know what they were. In reply Christ stated four negative commandments in the order given in Exodus 20:13–16 and Deuteronomy 5:17, and then gave the positive commandment of filial piety, which precedes these four in the second tablet of the commandments. Finally he added the positive precept of Leviticus 19:18: ". . . and love your neighbor as yourself."

The young man's answer was so spontaneous that it seems to have burst out in sorrowful impatience. Probably he interrupted our Lord as he was reciting the commandments. He could say in all truth that his integral observance of the Law had brought him no peace of heart. He was longing for something more, all unaware that he stood at that moment at the threshold of the Messianic kingdom (Gal. 2:21). In the light of this inner drama, his cry: "I have observed *all* these things; what am I still lacking?" is almost tragic. This humble confession of inadequacy and imperfection must have touched Christ's heart. Our Lord was already awakening him to a sense of God and suggesting to him the courageous fidelity that is the condition of all spiritual victories. Would the young man be drawn to him by the Father (Jn. 6:37–40)?

## Agape in the New Testament

Would he be called to perfection in the spirit of the New Law (Mt. 5:48)? The youth felt his own emptiness and desired to fill it. Jesus, with an exquisite responsiveness, gave him the means: If you truly desire perfection—completion—fulfillment—give up your riches and become my disciple.

In its demands for detachment from this world's goods, the passage is an exact parallel to the Sermon on the Mount, yet it does not seem at first sight to correspond to the Sermon's criterion of perfection for Christ's disciples, charity toward neighbor (Mt. 5:43–48). Two difficulties are apparent. First, our Lord had proclaimed the new justice to be an imitation of God, especially of his universal charity, but here perfection is identified with renouncement. Secondly, he had extended the precept of love to include service of our enemies as well as of neighbor, but in speaking to the young man he repeated without comment the Mosaic commandment of love of neighbor *as self*.

This second point is the more important. In unexpectedly adding the precept of love of neighbor to his enumeration of the official commandments, Christ revealed the great importance he attached to it. Furthermore, if the young man really did interrupt Jesus, as seems probable, he prevented him from explaining his concept of this love. Nonetheless, Christ's including the precept of fraternal charity confirms that it is, under the New Law, a means of attaining eternal life. Finally, his words were not an instruction to a large group, but the answer to a precise question, formulated according to the psychology of his individual questioner.

These considerations, however, do not alter the fact

## Agape in the Gospel of St. Matthew

that this important exposé of eternal life, and of perfection and the indispensable means to attain it, does not seem to give love of neighbor the primacy reserved for it in the charter of the kingdom of God. Fraternal charity yields to effective poverty. Since St. Matthew is the only synoptic writer who says that Jesus quoted Leviticus 19:18, some commentators have taken the text for a gloss by the Evangelist, ". . . a supposition which has cost him many reproaches. As early a writer as Origen doubted the text's authenticity on the basis that the young man, who had already 'observed all these things,' had therefore already accomplished the unique precept of the New Law, and therefore had already reached perfection. But according to St. Thomas there is a love according to the common way and a love of perfection. Modern critics object that by citing Leviticus 19:18, Christ departed from the Decalogue. As if this departure would not be the best proof that Jesus really did say the words, or at least that they come from a very ancient source! A correction would surely have limited the text to the commandments, well-known to all the Jews. If Jesus added this gloss, he did it to place his candidate for perfection in the way of perfect charity, leading to effective detachment" (M. J. Lagrange, *in h. l.*).

This interpretation is also given, according to the Latin pseudo-Origen (*PG* 13:1393–94), in the *Gospel according to the Hebrews* or the Aramean *Gospel of the Nazarenes*: "The second of the rich men (*it saith*) said unto him: 'Master, what good thing can I do and live?' He said unto him: 'O man, fulfill (do) the law and the prophets.' He answered him: 'I have kept them.' He said unto him: 'Go, sell all that thou ownest, and distribute it

## Agape in the New Testament

unto the poor, and come, follow me.' But the rich man began to scratch his head, and it pleased him not. And the Lord said unto him: 'How sayest thou: I have kept the law and the prophets? For it is written of the law: Thou shalt love thy neighbor as thyself, and lo, many of thy brethren, sons of Abraham, are clad in filth, dying for hunger, and thine house is full of many good things, and naught at all goeth out of it unto them.'

"And he turned and said unto Simon his disciple who was sitting by him: 'Simon, son of John, it is easier for a camel to enter in by a needle's eye than for a rich man to enter into the kingdom of heaven'" (*The Apocryphal New Testament*, translated by M. R. James, Oxford, 1955, p. 6).

Helping the poor is part of complete observance of the commandments, especially of the commandment of fraternal charity. St. Jerome agreed with this exegesis, remarking that, if the young man had really loved his neighbor, he would not have been so disturbed at the invitation to sell his possessions and to give the proceeds to the poor. "For if the commandment: 'You will love your neighbor as yourself' had been carried into act, why then after hearing the words: 'Go and sell your possessions and give the proceeds to the poor,' did he depart sad, because he had many possessions?" (St. Jerome, *Commentarium in Evangelium Matthaei*, PL 26:142.)

This traditional exegesis is probably correct, since it both emphasizes the main ideas of the narrative and respects their shades of meaning. 1) Christ, wishing to be assured that the young man's aspiration to perfection was sincere, reminded him that the basis of all true spiritual life was the Old Testament morality of fidelity to the divine will expressed in the Law. 2) Christ cited only the commandments that concern one's neighbor. On his own authority he added to them the precept of fraternal love, which he considered the most important, the foundation of all the others. 3) When the young man asserted that he had been faithful to the Mosaic legislation—"I have observed all these things"—Jesus revealed to him the "perfection" of the kingdom of heaven to which he was obscurely aspiring. "What am I still lacking?" He lacked a love of neighbor true and generous enough to lead him to help the poor even at the price of all his material possessions. The accent is on mercy and service of the poor, an eminent form of charity. Christ went even further. To help the poor with all one's own resources is not enough; the highest form of charity is to follow Christ, dedicating oneself, freed from the necessity of caring for a fortune, to the apostolate, to the spiritual welfare of others. The final promise, "you will have an investment in heaven," echoes the more general "lay up for yourselves treasures in heaven" and should be interpreted in the same spirit (6:24); the demands of charity are without limit.

If the sacrifice of wealth is materially most important, it is so only in the order of means and is imposed as a preliminary condition to serve the ends of charity. Charity explains the meaning and development of the dialogue. The opposition between the young man's "Is there something good I can do?" and Christ's "If you want to be perfect" is understandable only in terms of two different concepts of perfection: one, a morality of obedience; the other, a dedication in love. For the young man, perfection was the juridical fulfillment of prescribed, distinct, and well-defined precepts that did no harm to others and honored those near him. Christ's perfection was an interior love ready to abandon all property and sacrifice itself to help the most unknown neighbor in material or spiritual need. How can one arrive at such detachment, except by understanding that God alone is good (v. 17) and by acting according to his example (5:48)?

## CHARITY TOWARD GOD AND NEIGHBOR, FOUNDATION AND INSPIRATION OF MORALITY IN THE KINGDOM OF HEAVEN

"Rabbi, which is the great commandment in the Law?" He replied, "*Love* the Lord your God with your whole heart and with your whole soul, and with your whole mind. This is the great and first commandment. But a second commandment is like it: '*Love* your neighbor as yourself.' On these two commandments hinge the whole Law and the Prophets" (Mt. 22:37–39).

This pericope, simple as it is in appearance, is really among the most mysterious in the Gospel, preserving something of the "enigmatic" character of the question and of its answer. The conversation took place during Christ's last week at Jerusalem, when the Pharisees, Saducees, and Herodians were intensifying their insidious attacks against him in the hope of catching him off guard and making him compromise himself. After a discussion of the resurrection of the dead that had reduced the Saducees to silence, a group of Pharisees gathered and planned a new attack.

One of them, a lawyer, who, according to the context,

## Agape in the Gospel of St. Matthew

was probably a doctor especially competent in exegesis, tried to trap our Lord by respectfully submitting his question to him: "Rabbi, which is the great commandment in the Law?" (v. 36). Some exegetes believe that the question was purely academic. This interpretation seems improbable; the Rabbis mention such a question only much later. Moreover, the seeming clarity and simplicity of the problem presented with such apparent candor by an enemy must have concealed a difficulty completely different from the obvious one. What was it?

The questioner, since he was a Pharisee-lawyer, saw in the Law both the basis for all religious life and the link between God and the just. For him and his party, the critical point about Jesus was his position toward the Torah. Some of the things he did, like working miracles on the Sabbath, or of the things he said, about purity for instance, showed that he excused himself rather easily from particular precepts. How did he understand the force of the Law's obligation? Did he establish a hierarchy among the commandments? Did he make a choice among them? Did he recognize the authority of Moses?

Avoiding the juridical terrain, Christ answered by quoting the entire precept of charity toward God (Dt. 6:5). He insisted: "This is the great and first commandment" (v. 38). None of the Pharisees could object to the statement, since adoration was the central article of the credo that each Israelite was obliged to recite twice a day and to wear written on his phylactery. Then Jesus added something he had not been asked for. He suggested to the lawyer that his question had been poorly

## Agape in the New Testament

formulated. There is not *one* great commandment; there are *two*. "A second is like the first: love your neighbor as yourself" (v. 39). This quotation from Leviticus 19:18 would not have been especially striking if it had not been introduced by the bold statement: "A second [commandment] is like it." To love one's neighbor is a commandment equal to the precept of love of God.

The meaning of the very ordinary word, "like" (*homoios*), so important in this text, cannot be easily determined. The word is used consistently in making *analogies* of the kingdom of heaven or in indicating a *resemblance* when one person is likened to another (Is. 14:14) or in bringing together two *comparable* sizes or qualities. It can mean (1) a remote resemblance (Ct. 2:9; Prv. 19:12; Jn. 9:9; Ap. 1:13, 15 etc.); (2) a similarity of nature, species, or category (Gal. 5:21) within which there are, nevertheless, considerable differences, such as woman being like man (Gn. 2:20), that is, proportionate and complementary to him; (3) an absolute identity (Wis. 18:11). Very often, however, the word, when used in the Bible, connotes excellence. When the Old Testament wishes to exalt a Patriarch (Sir. 44:19), a just man (Jb. 1:8; 2:3), the Kings of Israel (1 Sm. 10:24; 1 Kgs. 3:12–13; 2 Kgs. 18:5; 23:25), or God himself (Ex. 15:11; Ps. 35:10; 86:8) it declares: "Who is like you? No one resembles you nor is your equal. You are without a peer." Such uses of the word "like" suggest that the second commandment has the same nature or value as the first. It is analogous to the first so that, without being strictly equal, the two commandments constitute a special category of precepts completely distinct from

## Agape in the Gospel of St. Matthew

all others. They have a common excellence and universality; the nature of the two loves is identical.

Even in the most exalted exhortations of the prophets, the Old Testament had not gone as far, nor had the Sermon on the Mount itself been as explicit. Christ had revealed that the disciples who loved were truly sons of God, but their acting in imitation of their Father, sharing his sentiments and perfection, did not imply that the objects of charity, God and neighbor, were the same and equal. This sameness is a matter of moral equivalence, of course, since there could be no question of identifying persons so disparate as God and neighbor.

The equivalence may be understood in two ways. If the emphasis is on the object of our love, God considers the love we bear our neighbor (Mt. 25:31–46) as addressed to himself; faith and charity reach to God in the neighbor. From the point of view of the subject, the Christian loves because God asks it of him (Old Testament) and in imitation of God (Sermon on the Mount) whose own love has been infused into his heart (St. Paul). The second interpretation seems preferable. If the first were correct, there would be only one commandment—to love—but Christ maintained a distinction and hierarchy of precepts. The precept of love of God is first and greatest; the other is like it but remains second. The close relation of the two precepts can come only from the very nature of *agapan;* it is one love with two distinct objects: God and fellow creature, whether neighbor, enemy, or the needy. In each case, we wish the other's good, show our respect for him, honor him, and serve him. This love is deeply rooted in the heart of

## Agape in the New Testament

man and has force and extension enough to command his whole moral life.

A conclusion of this kind, based on the uses of *agapan* in the Greek Old Testament, is implied in our Lord's final words, recorded only by St. Matthew: "On these two commandments hinge the whole Law and the Prophets" (v. 40). The lawyer had asked for an exegesis of the *Law*. Christ drew his answer from the Pentateuch, but he stressed the dominion of the two great precepts of charity over all the Law's prescriptions and also over the prophets' teachings. The great precepts are the life and soul of the entire legislation and doctrine of the Old Testament.

In profane and biblical Greek the verb "to hinge" (*kremannumi*) means primarily "to attach," "to hang (up)" an object (cf. Ez. 15:13), usually arms or military equipment, but it also means the suspension of a man, like Absalom suspended by his hair or neck, parallels which are hardly clarifying for our text. It also has the meaning "to plant or establish" (Ez. 17:22). In Job 26:7 and in Isaias 22:23–24 it has the notion of stability and solidity and can be translated "to occupy a base of operations."

In this sense, love of God and neighbor is the *foundation* on which man's entire religious and moral conduct rests, as a door rests on its hinges. Destroy the foundation and the whole structure will fall. In the language of parable, as objects hung from a nail are firmly supported by it, so each action of the just man, or according to the Jewish mentality, each precept of the Law, is based on the commandment of love. The emphasis is on interior cohesion; whatever a Christian does because of a particular commandment he will do in the name of the love which impels him.

The image of a foundation is plainly too static. Rather, charity is like a single cause producing multiple effects, or a single spring generating many currents and branches. Just as we cannot imagine a river without a source to nourish it, so also we cannot conceive of a Christian ready to act by any "principle" but love. The Christian's every word and action reveal the love to which he is responding.

For this reason, it can be said: "On these two commandments depend the whole Law and the Prophets." A principle rich with virtualities, love contains and summarizes all Christian morality. Our Lord reduced all precepts to the two which really form but one. He opposed these two to the whole Law and Prophets, but only to unite them in an interior compenetration. A virtue's importance or a commandment's prescriptive value depends on its close "adherence" to love. That was why our Lord answered the lawyer's: "Which commandment is supreme?" by giving his question the sense, "What sort, what category is supreme?" His answer was charity toward God along with love of neighbor, which belongs to the same class. All moral legislation depends on and fosters charity. In contrasting charity's supreme importance with the legalism and formalism of his adversaries' ideas, Christ condemned casuistry. He unified all morality, first by basing it entirely on exclusive adoration and worship of God (religious morality), then by consecrating Christians to the service of their brothers in the name of the love they bear God (social morality), and finally by requiring of each soul a single basic attitude, a single interior disposition—charity (individual morality).

The remarkable thing is that Christ's point of departure for expressing his concept of love was the text of the Old Testament. The Rabbis had sometimes suspected this primacy of love, but only Christ's authority could impose it. He alone was qualified to interpret and fulfill the divine oracles of the former Covenant. It was in the name of this love for God and men that he would let himself be crucified, a gift no precept of the "Law" ever prescribed.

## The noun *agape*

### THE GROWING COLD OF CHARITY
### THROUGH TRIBULATION

Then you will be subjected to afflictions, put to death, and become the scorn of all the nations, because you profess my name. Then, too, crowds of people will lose their faith, and betray and hate one another. Many, moreover, will falsely set themselves up as prophets and lead many astray and *because lawlessness will be rampant, most men's love will grow cold*. But he that holds out to the end will be saved (Mt. 24:9–13).

Introduced by an account of the destruction of the Temple (Mt. 24:1–3), this section opens the great discourse on the collapse of Judaism and the fall of Jerusalem, which is a foretaste of the end of the world. The things destined to happen at the time of the national catastrophe will be reproduced, but more intensely, at the end of time. Just as the "beginning of the pangs" (v.

8) in Palestine would prepare the birth of a new age, the coming of Jesus in his Church, so also the moral and religious tragedy of the last days will be the prelude to the Parousia of the Son of Man.

Verses 4–14 describe the early phase of the drama: first the preliminary signs (vv. 4–8) and then the conduct of the disciples (vv. 9–14). The hatred of pagans and of Jews will burst out against the community gathered "in Christ's name" to adore, to worship, to love, and to be faithful to him. Christians will be tortured and condemned to death. Formerly our Lord had spoken of persecutions as a blessing (Mt. 5:10–12). Now, strangely, he presents them not only as an eschatological event preceding "the end" but also as the occasion of downfall for many. "Many will be scandalized," that is, will succumb under the effect of terror; they will defect. This result, so striking and unexpected, will certainly not be limited to the weak and to a few exceptional cases, but will extend to the apostasy of a great number, even of seasoned Christians.

Because of these denials of faith, the Christian community will break up. The primitive Church's unity in charity will dissolve in dissension. Worse, apostates will betray their brothers who have remained Christian and hand them over to the persecutors. "Brother will give up brother, and father will give up child to have them put to death. Children will rise against parents and secure a death warrant against them" (Mt. 10:21). "A man's enemies will be the members of his own household" (v. 36). A scandalous hatred of the disciples for one another will be added to the normal hatred of the godless for Christ's disciples (Jn. 15:19). Finally many doctors of

## Agape in the New Testament

lies will arise within the very Church and their preaching will add confusion of mind (Mt. 7:15) to discouragement of heart.

Persecution by the pagans; accusations and hatred within the Christian community; heresies, lies, and stupidities on the lips of preachers—these will be the excess and the mystery of iniquity forming a prelude to the Parousia. The use of "to be rampant" stresses the extension as well as the gravity of the evil. This verb, not found in the papyri, is ordinarily used in a good sense in the New Testament (Acts 6:1, 7:17, 9:31, 12:24; 2 Cor. 9:10; Heb. 6:14; 1 Pt. 1:2; 2 Pt. 1:2; Jude 2). Of itself it means "to make numerous, to become abundant, to augment," usually with a nuance of progress as in "to expand more and more." Taken in a pejorative sense, as it is in this context, it means "to be excessive." This is the verb the Septuagint uses to express the multiplication of sins and crimes, prostitution, infidelities, outrages (2 Kgs. 21:6; 2 Par. 36:14; Esd. 9:6; Jer. 37:15; Ez. 11:6, 16:27, 23:19; Os. 8:11, 9:7; Am. 4:4; Ps. 40:13), especially the increasing malice of men before the deluge (Gn. 6:5) and the depravity of Sodom and Gomorrha (Gn. 18:20). These examples help to make clear the extent to which lawlessness will rule at the end of time. It will increase and develop to the point of contaminating most Christians; its contagious encroachments will exceed all conceivable limits. The phrase "lawlessness will be rampant" means that evils will predominate in the Church.

The result will be the cooling off of charity. Nothing could be more natural, it might be said. Since the whole law is summarized in charity (Mt. 22:37–39; Rom. 13:9; Gal. 5:14), any lawlessness injures or dissolves this uni-

## Agape in the Gospel of St. Matthew

fying element. But what is the "charity" in question? The noun *agape* is used only twice in the synoptic Gospels, here and in Luke 11:42. It has no direct object in the text under consideration. According to the context (notice especially verse 13), it must refer to the great commandment of love of God in its Old Testament application, which is both general and particular: "fidelity, observance of the commandments, adoration and service of the one true God." (Wis. 3:9, 6:18; cf. *Prolégomènes* pp. 88 ff.) In the train of iniquity's victorious progress, many Christians will break the ties of the Covenant, commit transgression after transgression, abandon themselves to the contagion of vice, succumb to their persecutors' threats, and end in joining their enemies by apostasy. Salvation could be promised only to a confident and persevering fidelity (v. 13; cf. Mt. 10:22). Since *agape* toward God is inseparable from love of neighbor (Mt. 22:37-40), here there may well be an allusion to the weakening of fraternal charity too. In periods of trouble and of persecution apostates will betray friends and family, and loyal Christians will protect themselves by shameful means. Far from worrying about their brothers, they will betray them to save themselves. It would be impossible to exaggerate the gravity of this eschatological scandal, for most Christians will fall. The *agape* here so betrayed is the authentic expression of Christian life; in Christ's mind it is the criterion and living sermon of the Church (Jn. 13:35).

*Agape* will "grow cold." Commentators translate this metaphor literally, for it could hardly be made more explicit. In Greek, the verb means first "to breathe or to blow," then "to refresh, make cool." A change in tem-

*Agape in the New Testament*

perature may be beneficial or it may be fatal, as when one is frozen with fear or gripped in the chill of death. In the passage under consideration the verb has the most baleful meaning. Charity does not diminish or progressively weaken; it becomes extinct. *Agape* is like a fire; to love is to burn (Sir. 9:8). The spouse of the Canticles said that love's "flames are a blazing fire. Deep waters cannot quench love, nor floods sweep it away" (Ct. 8:6–7). When a fire grows cold, it is dead, extinguished. What the spouse of the Canticles declared impossible will happen at the end of time. Under the power of an all pervasive, victorious evil many Christians will lose their first charity (Ap. 2:4), and those who were living will become spiritually dead. In this immense trial, each Christian can accomplish his salvation only by obstinate perseverance. "He that holds out to the end will be saved."

## The adjective *agapetos*

The adjective "beloved," which is not used by St. John, occurs eight times in the Synoptics, each time referring to Christ. The accounts of Christ's baptism and transfiguration are closely parallel in the synoptic Gospels; hence we will analyze them together. It is noteworthy that the first use—at the beginning of the year 28 A.D.—of a derivative of *agapan* in the New Covenant concerns the love of charity the Father of heaven bears his son.

## THE DIVINE PROCLAMATION AT CHRIST'S BAPTISM

> This is my son, *the beloved (ho agapetos)*, with whom I am well pleased (Mt. 3:17; Mk. 1:11; Lk. 3:22).

None of the evangelists suggests what rite was followed when Jesus was baptized. The heavens opened or "split" (Mark), and the Spirit (Mark) or Spirit of God (Matthew) or the Holy Spirit (Luke) under a corporeal form descended upon him as soon as he had come up out of the water (Matthew). A voice was heard from heaven, God's dwelling place (Mt. 5:34), but, according to Matthew, who translates it into indirect discourse, it did not speak directly to Jesus. It was certainly heard at least by John the Baptist (Jn. 1:32–34), and perhaps by all the people. Its purpose was to manifest the dignity of the son of God. "This is my son, the beloved, with whom I am well-pleased."

These words recall Psalm 2:7, addressed to the Messias: "Thou art my son." They could be understood in the broadest possible sense to mean only an adoptive sonship or a moral bond created by choice between God and Christ. According to classical and Old Testament usage, however, the epithet "beloved" applied to "son" implies not only sonship in the strict sense of a child begotten according to nature, but an exclusive and transcendent sonship; the beloved son is the only son. This declaration of sonship is not the same thing as a recognition or a consecration of Christ as Messias; the words of God contain much more.

When the heavenly Father in person—"from the heavens" is a periphrasis of God—recognized Jesus as his beloved son, he intended to reveal to every soul free from prejudice that he had engendered his son as has every father his own child, and that the love he bears his son is given to him alone. Scarcely any difference exists between "the beloved son" and "the only-begotten son"; the heavenly Father proclaims that Jesus is divine.

To stress the solemn character of this open proclamation of God the Father is not superfluous. God revealed and proclaimed that Jesus was more than the son of David (Mt. 1:1), more than the king of the Jews (Mt. 2:2). This divine communication to men of the identity of Christ seems to be the principal and decisive element in the baptismal scene. In order to dissipate the ambiguity resulting from his son's joining himself to sinners (Heb. 4:15) like a penitent, God declared that Jesus had no need to be purified (Jn. 1:29). Even in his human condition, Jesus is his own son; the Father and son have the same nature.

Moreover, God accredited his son before men. He recognized his authority, his rights of dominion over the world. For us, the declaration that Jesus is the son of God is a declaration of his sovereignty. Since he is son, he is entitled to perform all the acts of his ministry. Not only has he plenary authority and liberty of initiative, but the Father himself definitively ratified the inauguration of his son's reign on earth. As St. Paul later expressed it: "God was *in* Christ, reconciling the world to himself" (2 Cor. 5:19). The person of the Holy Spirit intervened, not to "sanctify" Jesus or to fill him with graces, but to guide him in his ministry. The opening of the public ministry is intrinsically linked with this outpouring of the Holy Spirit, this royal charism of power and light, representing all the divine motion that would act

## Agape in the Gospel of St. Matthew

on the Christ-man as he lived out the accomplishment of his mission. The manifestation of the Spirit in a way that was evident to the senses was a sign and a declaration: Jesus, recognized by the Father as his only son, acts under the personal influence of the Holy Spirit; the salvation of men is a work common to the Holy Trinity.

In classical Greek, the tender love of the Father for his son would have been expressed by the word *storge*. The use of *agapetos*, "beloved," implies a respect that has a religious value here. God loves his son, not like a father bending down to his little one with a rush of warm feeling, but in strict equality and with the intention of honoring him. By intervening to proclaim Christ his only son, God exalted and glorified him before men (Jn. 12:28).

The Father's words explain what kind of love unites him with his son. "This is my son, the beloved, with whom I am well-pleased." The verb "to be well-pleased" (*eudokeo*) is somewhat vague and has a variety of meanings. How should it be understood? In the Septuagint it usually means "to consent, to approve, to take pleasure." The love it expresses is highly spiritual, since it is in parallelism with the verb "to wish or to desire" (*thelo*). This benevolence is active (1 Mac. 8:1). When God was pleased with his people or with those who feared him (Ps. 147:11, 149:4), he showed them his favor, delivered them from their enemies, and helped them (2 Sm. 22:20; 2 Par. 10:7; Ps. 40:14). When he was not pleased, he destroyed (Sir. 45:19). The verb also implies deference, since it was associated with the Greek verb "to bow oneself before another (*proskyneo*)."

Thus, Jesus was the object of the divine favor. Since

the declaration of sonship and of delight are closely linked, it can be concluded that Christ was the object of God's benevolence precisely as son, possessing all of the goodness and perfection such a Father could give. The son, since he is unique, is loved as no other. The Father's delight in him, essence of paternal dilection, extends through all time. From all eternity the Father is unchangeably united by love to his son and "finds his delight" in him. Because the son is eternally born, flame of the Father's fire, his perfect image, the divine delight coexists with this origin and permanent newness. But if the divine declaration is also a reference to Isaias 41:8, 42:1-4, it can be secondarily the paternal approbation of Christ's Messianic work, of the Suffering Servant who came to assume the sins of his people only to remove them by his cross, and of the institution of Christian baptism. God delighted in Jesus during all his life on earth, but especially at his baptism, his consecration to the work of the world's salvation. The Father accepted in advance the lifelong devotion of the son. We can, therefore, give the verb the juridical meaning it had in the papyri of Hellenistic times: "to give one's approval, to be agreeable to an arrangement, to consent to the clauses of a contract."

In context, however, the verb has a much fuller meaning. At Christ's baptism the Father approved his son and was "well-pleased" in him. "Well-pleased" expresses their agreement of wills, with a note of fidelity and joy. It refers, not to a collaboration between God and Christ in some activity about which they have the same plan, but rather to the unfaltering, unrestricted delight of the Father in his son, a delight that defines their intimate relationship. There exists a communion of love between God and him whom he named his uniquely Beloved (*agapetos kat'exochen*).

## THE DIVINE PROCLAMATION AT THE TRANSFIGURATION

> This is my *beloved* son, with whom I am
> well pleased. Listen to him (Mt. 17:5; cf. Mk. 9:7).

Exegetical tradition has correctly considered Christ's transfiguration the central event of his public ministry, since God's manifestation in Christ sums up the whole Gospel. Taking his favorite apostles, Peter, James, and John with him, our Lord climbed to the mountain top. He had no sooner begun to pray than he was transfigured before them. His face became radiant with light, his clothing brilliant; he appeared before them in marvelous splendor. The true form (*morphe*—Phil. 2:6) of the son of God was momentarily revealed. In the Psalms God clothed himself with light as with a cloak (Ps. 104:2); his brilliance was like the light of day; "beams of light came forth from his hands" (Heb. 3:4). Christ, who will come again in all the glory of his Father (Mt. 16:27), is in himself "the radiant reflection of God's glory and the express image of his nature" (Heb. 1:3). It was perfectly normal, therefore, that the divinity should blaze forth through the veil of his body, and that at least once during his life with the apostles he should show himself to them as he really was—in his majesty (2 Pt. 1:16; cf. Lk. 9:43)—as he would later appear to the seer of Patmos: "His face was like the sun shining in full splendor" (Ap. 1:16).

## Agape in the New Testament

While he was thus radiantly transformed, our Lord spoke with Moses and Elias, who had appeared at his side, until Peter interrupted to suggest that three tents be constructed. His interruption was itself interrupted: "He was still speaking when, suddenly, a luminous cloud enveloped them" (Mt. 17:5). God was present! His sudden coming is the culminating point of the episode. Yahweh never appeared personally, but manifested himself through the *shekinah*—the cloud, symbol of his presence (Ex. 50:35; Lv. 16:2; Nm. 11:25; 1 Kgs. 8:10; Is. 6:1, 4; Ez. 10:1–22; 2 Mac. 2:8) and of his protection (Ps. 105:39; Wis. 19:7; Js. 4:5 ff.). At Christ's baptism the sky had opened and the Holy Spirit had descended from it, but here the "magnificent" cloud (2 Pt. 1:17) was so close that it covered or enclosed those present. No wonder the apostles were "terribly frightened" (Lk. 9:34). They recognized the cloud through which God manifested himself in his Temple. This place of his presence among his people had become so sacred and removed from men that the high priest alone, provided with the blood of expiation, could once in a year enter the Holy of Holies (Heb. 9:7). God's presence was, therefore, much more plainly visible to the apostles on the mountain than it had been on the banks of the Jordan. His manifestation was closer, more intense, more solemn, and more active because this theophany was for the sake of a revelation. God came in order to speak. A voice "rang out" from the cloud (Mt. 17:5; Mk. 9:7; Lk. 9:35), or as St. Peter himself magnificently expressed it: "Out of majestic splendor there came this voice: This is my beloved son . . ." (2 Pt. 1:17).

Undeniably the voice had the same origin and nature

## Agape in the Gospel of St. Matthew

as the voice at the baptism. It spoke the same words. But did it have exactly the same implications? The Father reaffirmed the unique and loving relationship uniting him to his son: "This is my beloved son." So profound a truth could not be too often repeated. Its renewed statement would awaken men to this mystery on which salvation and access to heaven ultimately depend. Furthermore, God spoke, not to a man who humbled himself among sinners as he approached John the Baptist, but to the *Kyrios* (2 Pt. 1:16) in all the splendor of his divine power and glory. Jesus was not just the Messias; he was also the "only son," the true son, the son divine. Consequently, the delight of love uniting Father and son is on a plane of strict equality and, according to Matthew 11:27, of reciprocity.

Two things make clear the opportuneness of the Father's declaration on Tabor. First, the son would later be glorified a third time by the voice from heaven speaking just before the passion (Jn. 12: 27–33). Secondly, each synoptic writer introduces his narrative by an unusually explicit detail of chronology (Mt. 17:1; cf. Mk. 9:2; Lk. 9:28); the transfiguration took place after Peter's affirmation of Christ's divinity at Caesarea when Jesus had announced his approaching death for the first time: "From that time on Jesus began to make plain to his disciples that it was necessary for him to go to Jerusalem, suffer much at the hands of the elders, high priests, and Scribes, be put to death, and on the third day rise again" (Mt. 16:21; cf. Mk. 8:31; Lk. 9:22). From that moment, he was on the way of the cross, on his pilgrimage to Jerusalem (Lk. 9:51). St. Luke explains why Moses and Elias appeared: "They spoke of his departure from the

## Agape in the New Testament

world, which he was about to fulfill at Jerusalem" (Lk. 9:31), that is, of his approaching passion. An analogy exists between the Father's interventions at Christ's baptism and at the transfiguration. His first intervention unmistakably compensated the son humbled among sinners; on Tabor he exalted and glorified the son in his acceptance of all the ignominy of the passion. Both times he declared his love, and this assurance comforted Christ in the trials he would undergo. Clothed with glory and covered with the cloud, the suffering Christ was sure of the protection and all-powerful help of the Father who loved him infinitely.

The final clause, "listen to him" (cf. Dt. 18:15), is given by all three synoptic writers and should not be overlooked. The verb is a present imperative which demands continuous attention and obedience; it means, "Listen to him always." St. Matthew might have used the aorist imperative, as he did in 13:18 where Christ tells his apostles to listen then and there to the explanation of the parable of the sower. Speaking to the three apostles, however, God approved in one instant all his beloved son's preaching and especially his announcement of the passion. The apostles made no secret of their bewilderment and indignation at the idea of the Messias' death. "At this Peter drew him aside and began to lecture him. 'May God spare you, Master,' he said: 'this must never happen to you'" (Mt. 16:22). They had been waiting for the brilliant manifestation of his kingdom. Perhaps the terror they felt on Tabor (Mk. 9:6) came from the conversation of Moses and Elias concerning the tortures awaiting our Lord. At any rate, when they came down from the mountain, they were worried about the

## Agape in the Gospel of St. Matthew

return of Elias. Jesus told them that he had already come back in the person of John the Baptist, and that the passion of the Son of Man would not be delayed much longer. Finally, the three apostles chosen as witnesses of the transfiguration would be the same ones admitted to the sight of the agony (Mt. 14:33) where their eyes would sink in sleep (v. 37) as they did at Tabor (Lk. 9:32). Undoubtedly, the whole vision on the mountain —the apparition of Moses and Elias, the transfiguration, the cloud and divine voice—was for the sake of authenticating the Messias' sufferings and prophecy while it fortified the faith of the disciples. These purposes are the point of the narrative. The scandal in their hearts since Christ's announcement at Caesarea Philippi of his death gave way to the sure knowledge that this suffering Messias was the only son of God, infinitely loved by his Father. A Christ rejected by his people would still be loved by God, who will always honor his well-beloved. In other words, the heavenly voice asked the three apostles to trust Jesus to the very end, whatever happened. It gave them sure testimony of the divine authority and of God's love for his son. Even the passion must be understood within that mystery of love. Thus, the declaration on Tabor, even more than at the baptism, insists on the *agape* of the Father, unchangeable, always helpful, brooding over his Elect even unto death.

The three apostles understood this revelation perfectly after their enlightenment by the Holy Spirit at Pentecost. Peter, who had to strengthen his brothers in the faith and who loved his master so much, based his authority as eyewitness of Christ's majesty on the vision of the transfiguration (2 Pt. 1:16). John, the beloved disciple, recalled at the beginning of his Gospel that he had contemplated the glory of the Word made flesh. He understood the death of a witness to Christ to be a glorification of God (Jn. 21:19), just as the passion of the son was. James was the first apostle to shed his blood for the Lord and so confess his faith (Acts 12:2); he was the first, the model for all the others.

### THE AUTHENTIC CHARACTER OF THE MESSIAS

> "Behold, my Servant, whom I have chosen, my *Beloved*, in whom my soul delights" (Mt. 12:18; Is. 42:1).

By exalting mercy above sacrifice and by healing a man's withered hand on the Sabbath (Mt. 12:1-14; Mk. 2:23-3:6; Lk. 6:1-11), Jesus aroused the Pharisees' anger and hatred so thoroughly that they held a meeting to see how they could get rid of him. He was warned and left the neighborhood to avoid their violence. He continued to heal the sick, although he asked those he cured not to talk about it.

St. Matthew sees a sign of our Lord's great prudence in his refusal to quarrel with the Pharisees or to let his miracles be known. He comments on it by quoting the great Messianic prophet speaking of the Servant of Yahweh (Is. 42:1): "Behold my Servant, whom I have chosen, my beloved, in whom my soul delights . . . he will not wrangle . . . nor will his voice be heard. . . . The reed that is bruised he will not crush, or quench the smoldering wick" (Mt. 12:17 ff.).

This text would hardly need special attention, coming as it does after the Father's solemn declarations at the

## Agape in the Gospel of St. Matthew

baptism and transfiguration, except that it expresses the lucid insight of the Evangelist and of the primitive Church into God's singular love for the Messias. The Septuagint version read: "Jacob, my servant, I will uphold him; Israel, my chosen one, my soul delighteth in him." St. Matthew rejected this translation's interpretation of the word "servant" as collective and turned to the original Hebrew, which does not mention Jacob or Israel. It concentrates on the very person of the servant (cf. Is. 42:4): "Here is my servant whom I uphold, my chosen one with whom I am pleased." Neither the original nor the translation, however, mentioned charity. Matthew passes over the idea of "support" or "holding" by God and instead gives the primitive and traditional idea of the election of the Messias by the words, "whom I have chosen." He introduces the expression, "my beloved," probably from the Father's words at the baptism. This love changes "servant" from mere Messias to God's own son. This is a beautiful example of the enriching and Christianizing of the Old Testament by the New Revelation. Jesus was thenceforth identified as the privileged object of divine love. Nothing could be more natural or less equivocal. The identification amounts to an official title: Jesus is the one whom the Father loves. His love is of so special a quality that St. Matthew found the verb "to accept willingly, to welcome" (*prosdechomai*), used by the Septuagint, much too weak. The verb was appropriate for a chosen one, but here the question concerns the Father's predilection for the son he engendered. St. Matthew chose the Greek verb *eudokeo* to express a love full of delight and joy.

Even transformed by St. Matthew, however, the verse

*Agape in the New Testament*

does not at first seem particularly adapted to the context. Certainly St. Matthew was not stressing the "Suffering Servant" idea. A closer study of Matthew 12, which could be called "The Struggle with the Pharisees," shows that Jesus, already rejected by the elite of Israel, had been excommunicated from the synagogue, practically speaking. He was forced to go away. Does this not suggest that the chosen people had lost the right to their title, "Servant of God," by their rejection of Christ? The title with all its privileges would pass to the new people who were being established and who would be faithful to God's chosen Servant, his well-beloved. This interpretation gives universal force to the prophetic title already accomplished: ". . . thus the prediction made through Isaias the Prophet was to be fulfilled: *Behold my servant . . . my beloved.*" At the baptism and transfiguration the Father had declared his love for Jesus and in exalting him had rectified his son's humiliations. St. Matthew contrasted the hatred of the Jewish authorities with the love and delight of God; the persecuted fugitive is the *agapetos*, the Father's beloved one.

St. Matthew develops this identification of Jesus into a portrait of him as radiantly unassuming, full of a perceptive tact that touched men's hearts. Jesus gave in and fled from the Pharisees because he would not give himself to quarreling and to violence, but he did not sink into silence or disappear into the desert. He kept on preaching, but more discreetly than ever, making his point through parables. "The reed that is bruised he would not crush, or quench the smoldering wick." What does this mean? Surely that the Savior gave himself to

## Agape in the Gospel of St. Matthew

the search for the sheep of Israel with gentle goodness and great respect.

He was himself the first to fulfill the beatitude of the meek who will inherit the land (Mt. 5:4). He thus gave hope to all nations. His meekness will earn the victory (Mt. 12:20). The son, so nobly loved by God, loves men in a most exquisite way. His Father's love for him lives in him, and he bestows this same love on men. He has truly received the divine Spirit (*pneuma*, v. 18). When the Father proclaimed his delight in his well-beloved on these occasions, he did so precisely because he saw his son consecrating himself with a great and tender love to the salvation of all. St. Matthew saw the public ministry in its most concrete form as a manifestation of the Lord's *agape* and a proof of the authenticity of Christ's mission. "Behold my servant, whom I have chosen."

## Conclusion

### GOD'S LOVE FOR HIS SON

The word and concept, "charity," appear for the first time in the New Testament at the proclamation of Christ's divinity (Mt. 3:17). Even before the son of Mary had shown himself in Israel and purified his Father's house, God made the most important of all revelations to the world. On the banks of the Jordan he named Jesus his son and his *agapetos*, his beloved. Clearly, *agape* exists in God; it is the force uniting the two divine Persons unchangeably, from all eternity. The Father loves his only one, not out of condescension or mercy, but because

## Agape in the New Testament

his all-perfect son is an adequate object of his love. Jesus is "lovable" in himself. God's "delight" necessarily reaches out to him, and the word "delight" (*eudokia*) expresses the communion between Father and son. The heavens opened, the divine voice spoke, the Holy Spirit descended —all to let men know this essential mystery of the life of the Trinity. God has an only son, with whom he lives united, since the Incarnation, by a love of charity.[2]

The second proclamation of this love, on Tabor (Mt. 17:5), is related to Christ's passion. Jesus was ordained to suffer, but he received then and forever the assurance of his Father's infinite love. God would not abandon him during his ordeal. Divine love revealed itself as always attentive and unchangeable; *agapan* expresses a love that never wavers. Moreover, God chose to reveal his love for his son as Jesus was about to consummate the work of man's salvation. Jesus is the object of his Father's delight precisely as crucified. Because his son suffered, God glorifies and exalts him, his *agapetos*.

Another passage (Mt. 12:18) confirms this interpretation of the Father's intervention. Here St. Matthew contrasts the Pharisees' hostility and rejection of the Messias with the declaration he sees in a passage from Isaias of God's love for his persecuted son. In presenting Jesus as "the beloved," St. Matthew demonstrates the authenticity of his mission. The faith of the Church added a new, decisive characteristic of the Messias to those already sketched in the Old Testament; he is the son of predilec-

[2] It cannot be overly stressed that all eight uses of *agapetos* in the Synoptics apply exclusively to Jesus as Son of God. *Agapan* and *agape* have various subjects and objects, but only Christ is perfectly *agapetos*. He is unique in the order of love just as he is in the order of sonship.

## Agape in the Gospel of St. Matthew

tion. Jesus is he whom the Father loves. Furthermore, St. Matthew conceives his entire ministry as a manifestation of a charity which is at one and the same time active, tender, attentive, and completely kind. He implies that God's well-beloved son is himself charity and that he loves men.

### THE LOVE OF MEN FOR GOD

The life of the members of the new kingdom is conceived as an appropriation to a Person, a belonging to God, and hence a service; to love is to serve (*agapandouleuein*, 6:24). "To love," understood as "to adhere willingly" to God, keeps the meaning it had in the Septuagint: "to love religiously, to adore." "To serve" specifies this consecration as exclusive and definitive. Taken as a whole, the logion demands attachment to God in expressed, exclusive fidelity as well as in faith and love. From the moment the Christian acknowledges and adheres to the true God, he becomes his liege man, bound to serve him with all his being. This idea contains the essence of New Testament charity. It is much more than a consecration of activities; it so seizes the very heart of man that it permeates all his thoughts and affections. He despises other goods, particularly money. Where his treasure is, there his heart will be. The heart, symbol of union and gift, cannot love and serve two masters at once. This profound idea proclaims the impossibility of a divided spiritual life and condemns the worship of any kind of idol. More important, it places the fundamental root of the liberty of God's children in *agape*.

## THE LOVE OF CHRISTIANS FOR OTHER MEN

From the time of the Sermon on the Mount Jesus very forcefully laid down the double commandment of love of God (Mt. 6:24) and neighbor (Mt. 5:43-48). St. Matthew expresses Jesus' five uses of the Aramaic "to love" by the Greek *agapan*. His explicit reference to Leviticus in Matthew 5:43 shows that he intended to keep the religious sense *agapan* had in the Old Testament. It conveyed the will to do good, expressed in respect, kindness, and service. But Jesus intended more than that; he evoked the Old Testament's authority only to pass beyond it. His morality was inspired by a new spirit. Now, charity has no limits. "Neighbor" is not family or compatriot or someone of the same religion; charity reaches enemies and the poor, whoever they are (Mt. 19:21). It includes absolutely everyone. Its motive for loving is that God loves, God who is absolutely good (Mt. 19:17). As Father of all men he gives his gifts to all men; thus, we his children must love everyone he loves and give them our gifts whenever we can. If we cannot give them something, we must at least pray for them. The providence of God our Father is the secret of Christian love's universality (cf. Mt. 29: 8-9; Gal. 3:28), especially in its most eminent form, compassion for the poor.

Since Christians must reproduce the quality and dimensions of God's love, they will try to know his love in the examples Christ gave. The Father's love is universal, individual, and generous. God knows each of his children (Mt. 6:4, 6; 10:29, 31); he does not forget a single one of them (Mt. 18:10). He knows in advance what they need (Mt. 6:8, 32) and wants their true happiness

## Agape in the Gospel of St. Matthew

(Mt. 5:3–10). Since "the Father in heaven" is all-powerful, the best thing the charity of Christians can do is speak to him on behalf of other men, even of their persecutors. Their love of neighbor will immerse itself in the divine love and become one with it. They will come to understand how they can and ought to love men as God loves them. Our heavenly Father has only one object worthy of his love, Jesus, his uniquely beloved; in him he is well-pleased. The rest of men are enemies; they are wicked and repulsive, without any apparent lovableness. God loves them, not because he takes delight in them, but out of generosity and kindness. Christians will love them in the same way, by showing them a love filled with respect and generosity. They love a neighbor, not for some good they believe concealed in him waiting to be brought to light, but because God loves him. Their gift, like God's, is purely gratuitous.

The resemblance between God's universal kindness and the Christian's desires and actions will grow more and more exact and bring about a new and mysterious relationship between them. God becomes the Father of Christ's disciples in a special way. He is a model whose characteristics his children reproduce, but he is also a true father who adopts as beloved sons those in whom he recognizes himself. Similarity of feeling and of acting results in a familial union; more precisely, it presupposes this union. No one can love his neighbor with charity unless he is God's adopted son; at least the apostles understood the divine sonship of Christians in this sense. Jesus implied this sonship in the Sermon on the Mount when he said that we cannot love and do good to all men indiscriminately unless we have, as sons, the same love

## Agape in the New Testament

God has for them. Charity, thus conceived, is a superhuman plenitude and perfection. God has this charity, and all who love their brothers with charity are perfect as their heavenly Father is perfect.

### THE DEGREES AND DEATH OF CHARITY

To love one's neighbor is not just a lofty ideal or a work of supererogation, but a true commandment. Its observance is required for eternal life (Mt. 19:16–21). Nevertheless, at the Lord's invitation to a higher perfection, all possessions may be given up for the poor. In other words, the fundamental consecration to the service of God which *agapan* desires (Mt. 6:24) involves a corresponding act of mercy and of service toward neighbor. Loving God perfectly demands freedom from every hindrance that will prevent the Christian from belonging to him exclusively; hence the Christian unhesitatingly renounces riches in favor of the poor. He loves his neighbor not just *as* himself but *more* than himself. The act of charity is a gift, and the more elevated this "virtue," the more complete the gift. Love of neighbor follows the same rhythm and can reach the same heroism as love of God. *Agape*, despite the difference in its two objects, is unique, founded only on the consideration of God's goodness. The man who becomes voluntarily poor for God's love enters a closer relationship with Christ, and then with the Father, whose privileged son he has become. There are degrees in *agape*.

Only the excess of iniquity at the end of time can account for the possibility that charity, a stable love, made to endure, can perish. Jesus declared that the scandal of

## Agape in the Gospel of St. Matthew

prevailing evil will chill the charity of many, even within the Church. Disciples will break the bonds uniting them to God and to their brothers (Mt. 24:12). The flame of *agape* must be fed and fanned by fraternal "edification"; it can thrive only in a favorable atmosphere. Nothing diminishes it faster than the chill of the brutal hatred of the majority. This "refrigerated" atmosphere can be resisted only by absolute and constant fidelity.

### THE MORALITY OF LOVE

A few days before his death our Lord summarized all his teaching and clarified its spirit. He reunited in a single category the two precepts, love of God and of neighbor, which had been separated when the Old Law was promulgated (Mt. 22:37–39). He declared them to be the basis of all the legislation and moral doctrine of the kingdom of heaven; they summarize all religion. They are transcendent because they are above and beyond "all the Law and the Prophets"; conversely, however, "all the Law and the Prophets" depend on them for their binding force and religious significance. When the Christian is trying to correct himself in relation to God, to his neighbor, or to himself, he will probably have to adopt some new attitudes or activities, but the inspiration of his diverse decisions will always be charity, the single rule of thought and of action. Should various duties conflict, charity will resolve the problem. A good quality is a virtue only insofar as it arises from *agape*.

It goes without saying that such a conception was a complete innovation compared with the anthropocentric paganism summarized in Protagoras', "Man is the meas-

## Agape in the New Testament

ure of all things." Christ made love of God and of neighbor the measure of human action. He effected a considerable modification even of the revealed morality of the Old Testament. Charity there was chiefly adoration of God and fidelity through obedience. In assimilating devotion to neighbor to this consecration, Jesus added an affective element to the chiefly "religious" idea of *agape*. If love for the poor is of the same nature as the love that unites one to God, it must be more than worship and praise; it becomes a love of the heart. God is a father in plain fact, and Christ's disciples are his children, who must love their brothers. Just as God acts through love toward men, so also Christians will show their love of neighbor in a thousand different ways. Their whole morality is "suspended" from that love.

CHAPTER II

# Agape in the Gospel of St. Mark

St. MARK, who does not record the Sermon on the Mount, never uses the noun *agape* and uses the verb *agapan* only five times. The last four of these uses are in the pericope dealing with the great commandment (Mk. 13:30–33), which is parallel to Matthew 22:37–40 but does not have the same doctrinal implications. The first and characteristic use of *agapan* is in the story of the rich young man (Mk. 10:21).

## The verb *agapan*

### THE LOVE OF JESUS FOR THE RICH YOUNG MAN

Jesus looked at him intently and *loved* him (Mk. 10:21).

The episode of the fortunate young man, called to sell his goods to follow Jesus, is parallel to Matthew 19:16–30 and Luke 28: 18–30, but St. Mark does not include love of neighbor in the list of commandments required for entrance into eternal life. Mark is the only evangelist to add that when the young man answered, " 'Rabbi, I have kept all these from my youth,' Jesus looked at him intently and loved him. Then he said to him: 'One thing is still wanting to you. . . .' "

This is the only place in the synoptic Gospels where *agapan* is used either in a simple narrative or to express what Jesus himself felt. Its meaning seems clear from the context. There are three closely-linked, successive moments in the dialogue. The young man asserted that he had been *faithful* to all the commandments, Jesus *looked*

## Agape in the New Testament

*intently* at him and then *loved* him. Christ was visibly surprised and impressed with the young man's integral and persevering obedience to the Law. His expression changed after the youth's declaration of fidelity, and without having anything of the curious or impertinent, his look must have become more attentive and more personal. Holding the young man's gaze, Jesus looked deep into him and saw that the fundamental disposition of his soul was good. He assured himself that his answer had not been light or boastful. At the end of the searching examination of his heart, Jesus was unable not to love the young man whose sincere and exceptional attachment to God he saw and admired—*he loved him.*

Yet the translation, "Jesus loved him," is not enough, nor is understanding *agapan* as a simple interior affection drawing Jesus to the pure and earnest young man. The Evangelist does not intend to reveal Christ's feeling from within; he is only transcribing what St. Peter, an eyewitness, observed as Christ's sudden affection became apparent in certain exterior signs. *Agapan* always expresses a manifest affection, a love that displays itself in action. There must have been a very noticeable show of affection, of loving sweetness, not only in Christ's look, but also in his voice and in his whole attitude.

It could be understood that, "Jesus, looking at him, made a gesture of friendship toward him" (H. Pernot, *Pages choisies des Évangiles,* Paris, 1925, p. 155), but it would be temerarious to suppose, as many modern writers have, that Jesus "caressed him," although that sense of *agapan* is well represented in profane Greek. Certain commentators have understood that Christ kissed the young man, as Rabbis embraced a disciple who had given

## Agape in the Gospel of St. Mark

a very good answer. Although the noun *agape* soon came to mean the liturgical "kiss of peace," the verb *agapan* did not have this meaning until much later.[1]

The error or at least hazardous character of these exegeses arises from a confusion between *agapan* and *philein*. It is not said that Christ felt a tender affection, much less friendship, for the young Israelite. The first meaning of *agapan* in biblical and profane Greek is "to esteem" and even "to admire." The quality of soul of the young man, whose generosity was already proved by his fidelity to God, filled Christ with respect. He *warmed* to the good he discovered, and he *showed* his esteem by treating the young man more cordially. The words of St. Mark: "Jesus looked at him intently and loved him," are a turning point in the dialogue. When the unknown young man had run to Christ and knelt at his feet, he had received the cold, almost severe answer: "Why do you call me good? Nobody is good, except one alone—God! You know the commandments." In the youth's reply Christ discovered a profoundly religious and humble soul, a soul that remained unsatisfied. He was conquered by its fervor and he welcomed the boy warmly. *Agapan* here certainly keeps its original meaning of hospitality, "to receive cordially." From then on, Jesus treated his questioner gently, with unusual kindness and an "exceptional courtesy," as Clement of Alexandria understood (*Quis dives salv.*, PG 9:613). His face must have lighted with a smile of approval and of encouragement that invited the young man to confidence; *agapan* often has a nuance of spontaneous delight.

---

[1] If Jesus' gesture had been a kiss, St. Mark would have written *katephilesen* or *enankalisamenos auton*.

## Agape in the New Testament

Christ's respectful affection is described principally to explain what happens next. The Lord, having received all power from his Father, proposes a privileged place in his kingdom to the young man. He invites the youth to follow him. *Agapan* contains the Septuagint sense here —"divine choice." Just as the Christ-man was surprised by the faith of the centurion and admired him because of it, so also his discovery of the young man's worth caused an attachment which showed itself in the gift of grace. According to St. Mark, Christ's love explained the youth's vocation.

The outcome, however, is disappointing. The young man went back to his earthly riches. He—called into the joy of his Lord—went away sad. The other disciples, who left everything, received life eternal (Mk. 10:28-30); this disciple was not interested in the love of predilection that Christ accorded him. His great refusal is one of the most poignant scenes in the Gospels.

### THE GREATEST COMMANDMENT IS TO LOVE

"Which is the very first commandment?" Jesus answered: "The first is this: 'Listen, Israel, the Lord our God is one Lord: therefore *love* the Lord your God with your whole heart, and with your whole soul, and with your whole mind, and with your whole strength.'

"A second commandment is this: '*Love* your neighbor as yourself.' Greater than these there is no other commandment.'" "Very well, Rabbi," replied the Scribe; "you are right in saying that he is one and there is none other but he. Moreover, to *love* him with one's whole heart, and with one's whole mind, and with one's whole strength, and to *love* one's neighbor as oneself is more precious than all the burnt offerings and sacrifices" (Mk. 12:30-33).

## Agape in the Gospel of St. Mark

The question about the greatest commandment and Christ's answer to it have already been discussed in the analysis of Matthew 22:34 ff. (cf. *supra* pp. 26–32) Luke (10:25 ff.) uses the episode to introduce the parable of the good Samaritan. Matthew sees it as the foundation of all New Testament morality, built upon charity toward God and neighbor. St. Mark's account, much more precise in historical detail but less elaborated doctrinally, probably reproduces the oldest, most authentic tradition.

Unlike the Pharisee–lawyer of Matthew, who came to Jesus with hostile intentions, Mark's Scribe was a man of good will. He deeply admired the Master whose wisdom and authority could silence his adversaries. A connoisseur of dialectic tilts, he was probably conscious of his own intellectual excellence and interested in an exchange as an equal with an eminent master. At least he proposed a question in his turn: "Which is the very first commandment?" (Mk. 12:28).

All three Evangelists record that Christ answered by invoking Deuteronomy 6:4 ff. and Leviticus 19:18—the two commandments of love of God and love of neighbor. Only St. Mark gives the complete citation in which a profession of monotheistic faith precedes the first precept of love: "Listen, Israel, the Lord our God is the only Lord." This clause gives not only the object of the love to be exacted but also its justification. Yahweh is the God of Israel, who has chosen the nation as his own people. He has revealed himself to them and filled them with good things and generous promises. Justice demands the return of love for love. This return is Israel's part in the Covenant, forbidding it to devote itself to idols or to other pagan gods; *agape* means adoration and fidelity. The precision "with thy whole heart, and with thy whole

## Agape in the New Testament

soul, and with thy whole mind, and with thy whole strength," demands totality. Toward the one Lord, love ought to be absolute; there is nothing in man to be reserved for himself. All his faculties, all his life are committed to God under charity's dominion. *Agape* toward God is not only the fulfillment of a precept and the performance of a duty; it is gratitude's fundamental desire, an exigency of nature. Moreover, since Yahweh demands his people's love and not their obedience or fear, love is clearly the sentiment closest to his heart. The formulation of the precept is itself a revelation of God's nature.

Given the exclusivism and the transcendence of the love of God, it is disconcerting that the Lord should add: "A second commandment is this: love your neighbor as yourself" (Mk. 12:31). Only Mark comments: "There is no other commandment greater than these." The union of the singular "no other commandment" and the plural "than these" maintains the distinction between the two precepts, but puts both of them into a special category. No other commandment equals them in importance, in excellence, or, consequently, in force of obligation. Even in extension they are unequalled, as St. Matthew clearly understood. It would be going too far to see in St. Mark's account the primacy of charity over every other virtue in the sense of St. Paul's 1 Corinthians 13, but it is clear that the Lord intended to raise the precepts of charity above the precepts whose value was so inflated by contemporary Judaism.[2]

---

[2] "The Talmud attributed the same reward to obedience to parents and to the removal of a bird's nest without taking the mother" (L. Pirot, *Evangile selon saint Marc*, Paris, 1935, p. 552). The obligation of wearing tassels at the corners of the cloak seemed just as strict as that of loving God.

## Agape in the Gospel of St. Mark

Jesus was not the first to teach the importance of charity nor even to unite love of God and of neighbor. In his teaching, however, the alliance is far more than an occasional thing. He stresses it as interpreter of the will of God, bearing his authority as Messias and as prophet, an organ of a revelation, not as any Rabbi might in responding to the turns of a casual argument. It has not been sufficiently noted that Christ defines the nature of fraternal charity in a completely new way by the constant union he establishes between the two precepts. It was already clear that charity extended to an enemy and to the sinner. The "neighbor" is not just someone near—a fellow countryman or a friend—but everyone, anyone. Neighbors are to be loved "as oneself," but God is to be loved without any measure. Jesus' literal and doctrinal association of love of the Lord and love of neighbor shows that love of neighbor is of the same type, of the same nature, as love given to God. This love is an attachment so total and definitive that it has the value of religious consecration. It spends itself in services and proves itself in fidelity. Love of neighbor prescribed by Christ is a profound and sincere gift of self. Far from being occasional and passing, it is constituted by constancy, so much so that the whole life of the apostle will be held in the bonds of charity. Charity does not consist of good intentions only; it is avid to give proofs of its love. A Christian can be defined as a man who devotes himself to his brothers. In some way, he belongs to them just as he belongs to God himself; in any event, the activities and modes of his love for them will be regulated and inspired by the same love that unites him to God. This is what Jesus explained: "Love one another as I have loved you" (Jn. 15:12), and St. Paul would practice: "I will most gladly spend myself and be spent to the limit for the sake of your souls" (2 Cor. 12:15).

The Scribe—whose reply only St. Mark has recorded for us—was enthusiastic about Jesus' answer, and complimented him on it: "Well said, Master" (Mk. 12:32). According to Semitic usage, he picked up Christ's words and correctly drew from their literal form the spirit Jesus wished to display. Charity, sum of the moral law, is more than law; it is "more precious than all the burnt offerings and sacrifices" (v. 33). In the Diaspora and after the destruction of the Temple such a statement would not have been shocking. Even in the Palestine of Christ's time a Rabbi might have said something similar, but it would have been more concerned with "works of charity" than with charity itself, and with meritorious and expiatory efficacy than with virtue and intrinsic worth. The Scribe in the Gospel saw that Jesus was not establishing a random hierachy of values—mercy above sacrifice—but was setting love in an order apart, superior even to the most sacred, the cult of God. More profoundly, the interiority of the morality of charity raises it above the exterior quality of works.

The Scribe showed unusual intelligence and religious intuition. Jesus, in turn, admired his wisdom (v. 28), his feeling for the primacy of charity. Let him behave accordingly and he will enter into the kingdom of heaven (cf. Lk. 10:28). Meanwhile, he is not far from it, and Jesus invites him to consider himself a proselyte who "draws near."

## The adjective *agapetos*

JESUS, BELOVED OF HIS FATHER, MARK 12:6.

St. Mark uses *agapetos* three times: in the baptism and transfiguration scenes and in the parable of the murderous vinedressers. "He still had a beloved son whom he sent to them last of all." Luke 20:13, in the parallel recitation, has: "I will send my beloved son." We will discuss both texts together.

This allegorical parable is the definitive element of the Jerusalem preaching and a prelude to the passion. It is the only parable, besides those of the sower and the mustard seed, to be recorded in all three synoptic Gospels. God is likened to the owner of a vineyard; the vineyard is the chosen people, who have been filled with blessings through his successive gratuitous interventions in history. The owner expects a revenue from his vine, recognition of his sovereign rights by docility to his prophets' messages, and obedience to his commandments.

God reaches his vinedressers through messengers. He sends one, then two, then three, and finally many other servants. The servants, literally slaves, are the Prophets and holy men of God in the Old Testament. Representatives of Yahweh, these "slaves of God" were men to be honored, clothed with a sacred character (especially Moses [Jos. 14:7; Ps. 105:26] and David [2 Sm. 3:18, 7:4]). Yet, from Elias to John the Baptist, they rarely received an appropriate welcome; more often they were despised and rejected, struck, insulted, even put to death.[3]

---

[3] 1 Kgs. 18:13, 19:1, 22:24-27; 2 Kgs. 6:31, 21:16; 2 Par. 24:19-22, 36:15-16; Neh. 9:26; Jer. 37:15; cf. Mt. 23:29-37; Acts 7:52; Heb. 11:36-38; Ap. 16:6, 18:20.

Jesus evoked the ignominy of this evil treatment which was renewed in a worse way with each mission from God. The proprietor does not seem to dream of becoming severe and of demanding reparation for the outrages. The vinedressers take his long-suffering for weakness and feel safe in continuing their abuses.

Such patience is so unlikely that it does not correspond to any human situation and must be a revelation of *macrothymia*, the divine long-suffering. God ignores the insult contained in men's disobedience or revolt; he does not impose respect for his sovereign rights. Rather than punish the guilty at once, he gives them time to be converted. The proprietor seems to trust the vinedressers. In spite of their continuing bad will, he ignores the past and sends servant after servant, trusting that a sudden change to good will may always be possible. No man would ever act in this way, but the choices of divine love are darkness to human wisdom (Is. 55:8-9). The first lesson of the parable is the revelation in God's patience and magnanimity of his extraordinary goodness. Jesus makes the divine charity known by showing the longanimity and untiring care of providence for the chosen people. In the face of man's incredible wickedness and equally incredible stupidity, God's generous love appears in a stark light under a tragic form. This is not just the rhetorical effect of well-chosen figures in a parable, but is truly the meaning of the facts of a millennium of history. Yet the divine patience, far from being exhausted or at an end, tries a most daring tactic.

All the servants' missions having failed, God decides to send his son—a resolution in which St. Mark sees pathos. The master of the vine always keeps the initiative.

*Agape in the Gospel of St. Mark*

He decides to send another deputation, but with a change in the quality of the ambassador. The new envoy will be someone on whom the vinedressers dare not set a hand nor even send back without an answer. If the vinedressers had received him respectfully, it seems that their earlier crimes would have been forgotten or tacitly pardoned. The words used of the last messenger show God's respect and love for him: "He still had a beloved son whom he sent to them last of all" (Mk. 12:6). Instead of a slave, the son is sent; instead of many nameless servants, the only, the beloved son. The expression, "beloved son," is materially identical with that of the baptism and transfiguration, but in the parable it assumes a special force. The beloved son cannot be just a privileged servant of God, nor even the Messias himself.[4] St. Mark states clearly that this son is the only son engendered by the Father; such a generation must be the eternal generation. If God sends his son on a mission as a "last one," it is because there is no possibility of sending anyone else. He is the only messenger who "still" remains. The unique, beloved son, the heir, can have no successor or replacement. More clearly than at the transfiguration, the designation "beloved" is related to the passion. There, as here, "beloved son" can be translated as "only son," but in the parable

---

[4] It would be impossible to overemphasize the Christological importance of this allegorical text; "one" in conjunction with "son" designates Christ as "only-begotten." Jesus is contrasted with the whole series of "servants," including Moses, the mediator of the Old Covenant. None of these had any personal interest in the vineyard. The new messenger has all the rights of the father; he is the only heir because he is the only son. In Luke 2:49 Jesus distinguishes the paternity of God from the paternity commonly attributed to Joseph; "I had to answer my father's call" is opposed to "your father and I" (v. 48).

## Agape in the New Testament

the emphasis is on the Father's exceptional love for his son. The Lord of the vine, who felt no hesitation in exposing additional servants to the most cruel treatment, now sacrifices the being dearest to him, his beloved. No doubt, he anticipates that the lawless vinedressers will respect his only one and be softened "by his kind dealings with them" (M. J. Lagrange, *in Mk. 12:6*). But he, the master of history, really knows very well the fate that awaits his son. He knows that his decision is a condemnation to death. "Never has any man, especially never any father, except in an extraordinary circumstance like war, had the heart to risk his son to such circumstances. For a father to do so, truly that father would have to be God and that son Jesus. . . . *For God so loved the world that he gave his only-begotten son!* He would send that beloved son alone after all the others, and the son would go courageously to the fate he knew. This is the simple history of our redemption, the poignant proof of the divine love for the Jews and all men" (L. Pirot, *Evangile selon saint Marc*, Paris, 1935, p. 544). "Beloved" is one of the key words of this story, which is more than a recalling of Yahweh's relations with Israel and a prediction of the coming passion. It is the theological explication of Yahweh's actions and of the passion; it reveals their secret—God has acted and will always act from love for his vine. He loves it so deeply that he treats it with unalterable patience and with unlimited generosity. He desires its good so truly that he decides to sacrifice his dearest one to it—his beloved. Even his only son is delivered up to the vinedressers.[5]

[5] Lord of the vine, servants, son, all the persons of the allegory exist and act because of the vinedressers. "The life of an only son

*Agape in the Gospel of St. Mark*

The last messenger, however, coming among his own, is not received (Jn. 1:11). The vinedressers, blind to the infinity of God's love, think only of themselves and of their chance of seizing the heritage. They kill the son. *What will the Lord of the vine do?* (v. 9). This question introduces the point of the parable; the Lord of the vine, who considers all their other misdeeds negligible, at last asserts his authority and rights. He is touched personally by the only crime that counts for him, the murder of his beloved. He will avenge the crime. His anger is in proportion to his love for his son. Allied to divine justice, divine love cannot forgive obstinate sinners. It is as severe when every last hope of conversion is lost as it was constant in mercy and in support while hope remained. God comes in person. He destroys his son's murderers and dismisses the shepherds of the Jewish nation (cf. P. Benoit in *Revue Biblique*, 1954, p. 140; G. Baum, *The Jews and the Gospel*, Westminster, 1961). He gives his kingdom to the Gentiles who will bear him fruit. His beloved will become the "cornerstone" (Ps. 117) of the new structure. He will rule over the Church.

Far from having been checked by the rejection of its first beneficiaries, God's love displays itself with greater glory in the redemption of all men and in the exaltation of Jesus.

---

is infinitely more precious than any products of a vine could be. Here, strangely, the synoptic writers all suppose the pre-eminence of the vine. It seems to be loved more than the son. We have made it clear that this could apply only to the allegory of the redemption" (D. Buzy, *Les Parables,* Paris, 1927, p. 412).

# Conclusion

### GOD LOVES HIS SON AND OTHER MEN

The reader of St. Mark's Gospel discovers that the God of Christianity is a loving God. He cherishes his only son uniquely and proclaims his love twice in solemn circumstances—at the River Jordan and on Mount Tabor. The parable of the murderous vinedressers completes the nuances of honor, pleasure, and attachment contained in the verb *agapan* in the synoptic Gospels by adding nuances of great worth and tenderness. The beloved son of Mark 12:6 is presented as especially "dear" to his father—it is this predilection that distinguishes him from the servants—so much so that the correct translation of *agapetos* in this context would be *carus*, and *caritas* in the precise theological sense of the word can henceforward be ascribed to God. A great innovation of the parable is the revelation of divine love by Jesus himself. The son knows he is the object of a special love. Because the parable is allegorical, Christ's docility to the mission of the Father can be understood as the expression of his deep love, a love that creates identity of desires. It is implied that the son, object of divine love, returns the same love to his father.

Besides loving his son, God loves men, especially the chosen people, manifesting the generosity of his charity throughout the centuries in freely given providential care of them and never-failing patience. All the relations of God with Israel are shown to be inspired by love, which reveals itself unmistakably in his deeds and gestures. This is the understanding Jesus gives of "sacred history."

JESUS LOVES OTHER MEN

St. Mark is the only synoptic writer to say expressly that Jesus felt a predilection for a person. Christ was filled with respect for the work of grace in a human soul by the fidelity to God's will of the young man in 10:21. He welcomed him warmly and treated him cordially. Since *agape* is a love that gives to those it chooses, Christ offered the young man a place and privileged role in his kingdom, the greatest gift he could have given him. God loves men, whom he fills with good things, and he has a unique predilection for his son, who not only returns love for love but also, whenever the opportunity offers itself, displays a striking "motivated" charity for the men who are the object of the divine *agape*.

CHRISTIAN CHARITY

Jesus asks his disciples to adore God and to be faithful to him, to love him with all their soul and all their strength (12:30–33). Authentic *agape* clings to the only true God. Deriving from faith, its first instinct is to proclaim him. Henceforth, however, it is known from St. Mark's Gospel that the God of Jesus is a loving God, and the charity of the believers is roused not only by the commandment and the revealed Word, but also by the realization of the divine goodness toward his chosen people, shown especially in the sending of his son. After this, "Christian charity" will no longer be synonymous with exclusive attachment, obedience, and service (cf. Mt. 6:24), but will be love properly speaking—preference. Christ's disciples are invited to love God above all else because he is infinitely lovable.

*Agape in the New Testament*

They are also invited to love their neighbor. The precept imposing this love is formulated with the same force as the first precept and is associated with it so closely that fraternal charity becomes elevated to the position of being the first of all duties. No other commandment, no other virtue begins to equal it in excellence or in gravity. Even acts of worship of God, religion's most authentic expression, are subordinated to fraternal love. A Christian can be defined as a person who loves. He will be Christian, with access to the kingdom of Jesus, in proportion as he is really united to God and to men by a love both interior and active.

# CHAPTER III

# Agape in the Gospel of St. Luke

St. Luke and St. Matthew each use the noun *agape* only once, but with different meanings (Lk. 11:42; Mt. 24:12). Luke uses the adjective *agapetos* only twice, but employs the verb *agapan* more than any other synoptic writer. It occurs thirteen times in his Gospel, six of them in the Sermon on the Mount.

## The verb *agapan*

FRATERNAL CHARITY

But to you who are listening I say: *love* your enemies; treat kindly those who hate you; bless those that curse you; pray for those that revile you. . . . Again, if you *love* those that *love* you, what thanks can you expect? Why, even sinners *love* those that *love* them. . . . On the contrary, *love* your enemies; do acts of kindness and lend without expecting any return. Then your reward will be abundant, and you will prove yourselves children of the Most High, who is kind to the ungrateful and the wicked. Be merciful just as your Father is merciful (Lk. 6:27, 32, 35).

St. Luke summarizes the Sermon on the Mount in twenty-nine verses. They correspond to St. Matthew's Chapters 5–7, which stress the opposition in Christ's teaching to the Law and to the justice of the Old Testament as they were understood by the contemporary Rabbis. Both writers modified the original sermon by inserting sentences Jesus spoke under other circumstances. Matthew's account, reflecting as it does Christ's attitude toward contemporary Judaism, is undoubtedly closer to

*Agape in the New Testament*

the original form of the Sermon. St. Luke's exposition is oriented toward his Greek convert readers, who were members of the lower classes of society. He "reconstructed" the Sermon more than Matthew did, and presented it more nearly unified. Most important, he has brought out its spirit more clearly by elaborating Christ's teaching on love of neighbor. This is his special contribution to the theology of *agape* in the New Testament.

Verse 27: Jesus, after choosing the twelve apostles destined to become the leaders of the New Israel, outlined the dispositions he required of them: "But to you who are listening, I say, 'Love. . . .'" The demand is absolute, and the challenging examples of the practice of charity that follow are its concrete commentary. The emphatic position of "but," followed immediately by "to you," forms a strong antithesis to the spirit of the world which our Lord had just condemned in four maledictions.[1] Christ's disciples had been proclaimed happy because of their poverty, hunger, tears, and persecutions. Next they were told to reach out to the thankless and hostile world by untiring, patient, and merciful love (vv. 27–38). Love is the only virtue required; it is the mark of Christ's disciple.

Luke omits any reference to the Pentateuch, and so presents the commandment of charity as the new and completely personal teaching of Jesus. Although our

[1] On the other hand, utterly wretched are you, the rich, for you have your comfort here and now. Utterly wretched are you who now have your fill of everything, for you shall go hungry. Utterly wretched are you who now are merry, for you shall mourn and weep. Utterly wretched are you when all the world speaks well of you; for so, too, the false prophets were treated by their fathers (Lk. 6:24–26).

*Agape in the Gospel of St. Luke*

Lord had not actually formulated his doctrine that way, what he said did contain a radical innovation which Luke understood and intended to emphasize. A comparison of his account of the Sermon with Matthew's account shows this intention at once. Matthew began with the beatitudes and composed the body of the Sermon of many extremely diverse logia: the salt and the lamp; the new justice; adultery; etc. He mentioned Christ's teaching on charity only as one maxim among others. Luke, on the other hand, conceived the charter of the heavenly kingdom entirely in terms of charity. The whole Gospel can be summarized in one word: the command, "Love!" Accordingly, Luke accentuated the word strikingly by placing it at the beginning of the Sermon proper. "But to you who are listening I say: love your enemies . . ." (v. 27). He repeated it in verse 35: "On the contrary, love your enemies. . . ." This verse is the "recapitulation" of the teaching; the entire section is to be understood, therefore, in terms of love of neighbor. In his Gospel, Matthew had simply glossed the imperative "love" with another imperative "pray" (Mt. 5:44). Because St. Luke was using the word for the first time in verse 27 and wanted to show its force, he added a series of synonyms or equivalents: treat kindly, bless (vv. 27–28), do acts of kindness (v. 35), be merciful (v. 36).

According to St. Matthew, Jesus opposed to the precepts of the Old Law a superior sort of justice—love of enemies as well as of neighbor. As St. Luke reconstructs the Sermon, Jesus singled out his disciples from the pagan world in describing them as characterized by charity, a charity he presented under its extreme forms and most difficult demands. In a world of the rich, the well-fed, the

## *Agape in the New Testament*

merry, and the admired, the members of God's kingdom will appear as poor, hungry, and wretched. Nothing could be more natural than for them to be bitter toward the more highly privileged and to try to get revenge for injustices they have received. In fact, they are hated and persecuted precisely because they are Christians. Their neighbors in this world are the enemies of their faith, and as enemies show their hostility in calumnies, curses, and all kinds of petty annoyances or real injuries intended to disturb and to harm Christ's disciples. Jesus asked his followers to respond to each display of ill will with a display of love. Another person's hostility only provides occasions for the Christian to show him over and over again how much he is loved. No injury or display of contempt can outreach the disciple's patient, gentle kindness. Jesus must have proclaimed vehemently: love, love, love! To misunderstand him is impossible. His disciples will respond to hatred with active benevolence. They will bless those who curse them, begging God's mercy for them; they will praise even their calumniators and try, at least, to honor them (cf. Lk. 1:64, 2:28; Jas. 3:9). When faced with jeers and slander, they will find an answer that pleases their enemies; such a reaction is perfectly natural to *agape*, which is always lavish with praise and honor. Even if hatred is so successful in its vexations and persecutions that the Christian has no freedom to respond as he would like to, he can always intercede with God for his enemies. Prayer becomes the only possible expression of his deep desire to do good to his enemies; it is patient charity's final victory.

Verse 29: "If someone strikes you on your cheek, present to him the other one as well; if someone takes away your cloak, do not stop him from taking the tunic also." The first example is doubly wounding, for it is both painful and insulting; Jesus was speaking of a violent blow on the jaw, not of a more or less gentle slap on the cheek. In the second example, he asked his disciples to give up willingly not only the *himation,* the unfitted cloak worn loosely draped around the body, but also the *chiton,* the undergarment worn out of modesty and sometimes more precious than the cloak.

Instead of putting the verbs in the plural as he did in the preceding and following sentences, St. Luke used the second person singular imperative, no doubt to suggest that these concrete examples are illustrations of a principle and are not precepts. The wicked man is not to be resisted; the injustice of his aggression has no bearing on the case. Charity assures the Christian that patience, which controls anger, resentment, and revenge, will triumph in the end. It would be inexact to say that Jesus was prescribing a "spirit" which ought to inspire Christian conduct. The only spirit he ever prescribed was the spirit of a son of God, with such a son's sense of values, beauty of soul, thoughts, and actions. In fact, in a particular case prudence might require an injured disciple to act in a way quite different from Christ's examples. What he intended to show by these paradoxical illustrations was the perfect self-mastery he expects from his followers. Only *agape* has this power of ruling a person completely, because it is inseparable from renouncement and sacrifice. No one can love his neighbor as a Christian should unless he is willing to give up his own pleasure, his own comforts, and even his own rights.

It would be incorrect, then, to explain these verses as

descriptions of a higher perfection proposed only as an ideal. To consider them as counsels and not precepts, to use a later terminology, would destroy the seriousness of our Lord's teaching. They mean that each Christian must be ready, whenever there is a need, to give up his most basic rights and necessary possessions. Jesus' command was for a *praeparatio cordis*, according to the expression of St. Augustine. The burden of the text is clear; charity, as desire for another's good, requires the sacrifice of one's own good. It knows no limit; a pardon is to be seventy-seven times repeated. If charity puts an end to its concessions, it will not be because it has reached the limits of its resources. Charity sets its own limits; none are imposed from outside by a difficult situation. When Christ's disciples yield to their adversaries, they yield out of charity. When they resist, they resist out of charity. The measure of love is love itself.

Verse 30 repeats the thought by generalizing it: "Give to anyone that asks you; and if someone robs you of your property, do not claim it." Casuistry, which seems to come instinctively to men, could suggest a way of refusing this heroism demanded by Christ: "Granted that one could be led to give all, it would be only wise to choose the recipient prudently and perhaps someday get back what was given." Jesus closed this loophole: "Give to anyone who asks you, and if someone robs you of your property, do not claim it." The word "anyone" is stressed in the first part of the sentence, and the context shows that "anyone" means particularly an enemy. Charity is generous to everyone indiscriminately, even to naturally unpleasant persons or to those who try to do harm. The second part of the sentence, directing

## Agape in the Gospel of St. Luke

the disciple not to reclaim later what he has once given away, means that charity always gives graciously and forever. The present tense in the verbs suggests an habitual practice or even a continuous giving. Charity is the steadfast virtue of Christians; its demands are constant, surpassing all others. Everything must yield to fraternal love, even the obligations of the external worship of God (Mt. 5:24; Mk. 12:33).

In comparison with the loftiness of this doctrine, the next exhortation seems modest indeed: "In general, do to your fellow men exactly as you wish them to do to you" (v. 31). We do not know who first called this "the golden rule" of Christian morality, but unfortunately it has become a traditional expression. It is found in all the commentaries on the text, but it would apply infinitely better to the precept: "Be perfect (merciful) as your heavenly Father is perfect (merciful)." To act toward others as we would like them to act toward us is simply a rule of ordinary decency, found over and over again in profane, Old Testament, and other religious literature.

Most exegetes explain that Christ's positive formulation of the precept is much more expressive than the negative turn his predecessors gave it. They have forgotten Calypso's touching avowal to Ulysses: "What I shall devise and what I tell you will be the same as if your great need were mine. . . . My heart is all pity" (Homer, *Odyssey*, V, 188). Homer's parallel text shows that Christ was speaking not of simple good sense nor of justice, but of the love that puts itself into another's place and wants his good as it wants its own. Most pagan authors, because they approve of magnanimity and of prudence, praise their heroes for refusing to return evil for evil.

Jesus wishes his disciples to act from a love of others that is as sincere and as inventive as their love for themselves. This axiom is a universal rule directing relations with neighbors. All the words and actions of the Christian are dictated and measured by *agape*. "Do to your fellow men as you wish them to do to you." "Fellow men" is very general. It includes pagans as well as Christians, but the context directs its application particularly to the importunate (v. 30), the aggressive (v. 29), and the antagonistic (vv. 27–28). We must answer their maltreatments, especially, in a completely opposite way, showing them that their injuries have made us happy. In other words, we are to meet hatred with love. "Do to them" in verse 31 corresponds to "treat kindly" in verse 27 (cf. v. 35); it is a commentary on the imperative "love" of verse 27: show all men a love like the love you wish them to have for you. It must be repeated that *agapan* is not a verb of cordial affection but of an active will to do good, full of respect and indulgence, and generous in kind services.

In verse 27 and the following verses, Jesus intended to clarify the attitude his poor, disgraced, and therefore blessed (vv. 20–23) disciples were to take toward their enemies (vv. 24–26). His intention is shown in verse 32 and the following, where he emphasized charity's universal extension and constant courtesies. Loving one's friends comes so naturally that it does not enter into the question here, but goodness to enemies is so excellent a thing that it is close to divine charity, the pure gift poured out on thankless men. It would be hard to find a clearer way of saying that the *agape* of Christians is disinterested. This section, taken as a whole, corrects any appearance of human calculation that might be read

## Agape in the Gospel of St. Luke

into verse 31: "In general, do to your fellow men exactly as you wish them to do to you."

"If you love those that love you, what thanks can you expect? Why, even sinners love those that love them. So, too, if you are kind to those that are kind to you, what thanks can you expect? Even sinners do as much" (vv. 32–33). The parallel construction of the two sentences suggests that "to love" (*agapan*) means "to be kind" (*agathopoiein*). *Agape*, always open and active, spends itself doing good in mercy. Our Lord intended to exclude the spontaneous devotion that sinners show their friends, precisely because it is instinctive, based entirely on natural liking. King Demetrius, for example, wrote to the Jews: "We have determined to do good to the nation of the Jews who are our friends and keep the things that are just with us, for their good will which they bear us" (1 Mac. 11:33). This kind of response is characteristic of justice or friendship (*philia*), but not of the *agape* of the disciples of Jesus. Love for enemies is different from love for friends, not only because of its greater extension but more essentially because it is outgoing and not self-centered. In loving those who love us, we may be loving only ourselves and using the others to satisfy our own needs. Perhaps our love for a kind neighbor may be sincere. Still, it is not necessarily manifest; besides, it does not have the element of rational choice essential to *agape*. This disciple of Jesus who is kind and generous to the indifferent or hostile is practicing the voluntary, purely gratuitous love which is authentic charity.

Plainly, the accent here is on *agape*'s disinterestedness, at least on the human level. Our Lord told his disciples not to look for anything on this earth in return for their devotion and kindnesses. It would seem that "charity" is somehow spoiled or weakened as soon as it gets any temporal return for its service.[2] Hence, the triple repetition of the question: "What thanks can you expect?" (vv. 32, 33, 34). The disciples are contrasted with "sinners" who give only when they are sure of a return: "Even sinners do as much." Actually, even the purest Christian love hopes for return and fruition. It waits for the granting of a favor or an expression of gratitude—but never from men. God alone rewards the love of charity, and superabundantly (v. 35; cf. v. 38). Christian beneficence must be disinterested in its deepest inspiration, and yet God considers whatever is done for neighbor as done for himself. He promises to repay those who love their enemies, if only their generosity is motivated by love for him. "And if you lend to those from whom you expect repayment, what thanks can you expect? Even sinners lend to sinners on condition that they recover the same amount. On the contrary, love your enemies; do acts of kindness and lend without expecting any return" (vv. 34–35[a]).

Jesus had proposed accepting blows and giving up one's clothing willingly (vv. 29–30) as examples of patient and generous love. Next he illustrated love's disinterested-

[2] However that may be, the whole economy of salvation is based both on the love of God for men and on the existence of a reward. God is just when he fulfills his promises; man, when he obtains what he has merited. Christ suppressed the earthly law of retaliation and replaced it with a celestial law. It is not man's to avenge or reward himself; only God has that prerogative. The worst possible deception would be to be repaid with the miserable, devaluated goods of this earth (cf. Lk. 6:24; Mt. 6:2, 5, 16). Men who have turned in their receipts here on earth run the risk of losing their claim to the goods of heaven.

ness by citing the lending of money without interest. As it was practiced in Israel, lending was not a fruitful financial operation for the lender, who charged no interest, but rather was a fraternal service, a form of almsgiving called forth by a neighbor's need. Only the impious "lend today and ask it back tomorrow" (Sir. 20:14). Sometimes when one of the just of Israel lent his compatriot money without interest, the debtor took advantage of his generosity and paid him back nothing at all, thus all but forcing him to refuse new loans.

Jesus told his disciples not to lend like the best Jews who asked only to get their money back intact, but to be willing to lend without ever getting anything back. The demand of absolutely stripping oneself is just as new and heroic as the examples of love already given. Obviously Jesus was not speaking on the level of the business world, nor of justice and prudence, nor even of the concrete exercise of charity. He was defining, in a Semitic way, charity's proper nature. It is absolutely gratuitous and completely self-forgetful, radically opposed to any expectation of repayment. There is no love without loss of one's self and one's possessions. On the practical level, the verses mean: "To give up only interest on a loan would not really conform to the total renunciation set up as an ideal. This renunciation is not a command here but a counsel. Those who object that 'lending' then becomes the same thing as 'giving' miss the nuance. Sometimes a person perfectly willing to borrow would blush to receive an outright gift. So one lends to him, glad to get repayment if it is offered, but ready to give up everything if there is need, *nihil sperantes*" (M. J. Lagrange, in *h. l.*).

*Agape in the New Testament*

Verse 35ᵇ: If the yoke of the Lord is truly sweet, the Lord cannot prescribe this heroic love of neighbor and total disinterestedness without promising great spiritual joys in return. Just as he had proclaimed the happiness of the poor, the hungry, and the afflicted who put their confidence in God, he now announced a double happiness proper to *agape*. There is a difference, however. The joy of the persecuted (v. 23) can be unconstrained even here on earth ("rejoice at such moments"). The great reward of the charitable, who have so much to suffer in the present, is reserved for the future ("Your reward *will be* abundant"). Only the happiness of heaven can furnish a superabundant compensation. Nevertheless, the effective practice of *agape* does earn an immediate, unhoped for reward; whoever sincerely loves his enemy becomes the son of God. He has acted like God, has displayed God's own spirit, and thus has drawn near to God; he has merited to be called and to be really his son. God is kindness itself, generosity itself, especially toward the ungrateful and wicked, toward those who do not acknowledge his kindness and who can be considered his enemies. It is by *agape*, preached from verse 27 on, that those who listen to Jesus can imitate the divine charity. *Agape* would seem to be directed only to enemies, as God's charity is to sinners and to the impious, but these two recipients of charity are mentioned only to stress the gratuitousness and kindness of this love which always seeks to give. Since *agape* is so generous, it will manifest itself best in the worst predicaments, when no self interest could account for its acts and no gratitude is to be expected.

Verse 36, "Be merciful just as your Father is merci-

## Agape in the Gospel of St. Luke

ful," concludes the entire passage. The present imperative "be (merciful)" corresponds to the command "love" of verse 27. In the light of the examples and explanations already given, particularly of God's own way of acting, the question is one not only of loving one's enemies but also of showing them this love in its highest form: mercy and compassion. In asking his disciples to love in this way, our Lord was appealing to their divine sonship. He commanded them to pity the misery of those who harmed them, because God pities the wicked and his children must resemble their Father. Finally, *agape*, a summary of the Gospel's moral teaching, is compared with God's generosity and seen to be the essential virtue of the sons of God. To love one's neighbor is to have at heart the same sentiments as the heavenly Father and to behave as he does. "Be merciful as your Father is merciful."

The element of mercy in charity, which has just been made explicit, is illustrated by one last practical application: "Do not judge, and you will not be judged; do not condemn, and you will not be condemned; acquit and you will be acquitted" (v. 37). This mercy goes farther than to the pardoning of personal offenses; it calls for a merciful judgment of the faults and failings of others. The *censor morum* is not Christian. Jesus must have been thinking of the Scribes and Pharisees arrogating to themselves the right to make hard, pitiless judgments in Israel. Their condemnation of the adulterous woman (Jn. 8:1–11; cf. Lk. 5:30, etc.) is a good example of their harshness. Christ forbids his disciples to pass any judgment on their neighbor's moral worth or conduct or ever to condemn anyone without first compassionately taking all

## *Agape in the New Testament*

the extenuating circumstances into account. If they are forced to judge, they must be swift to absolve, hopeful of acquitting, and ingenious in finding excuses for the accused so they can clear him (cf. Mt. 18:27; Acts 7:60; I Cor. 13:5; Jas. 2:13, 4:11, 12). Whoever exercises this kind of lenient charity will partake of the beatitude of the merciful—*Dimitte nobis peccata nostra, siquidem et ipsi dimittimus omni debenti nobis* (Lk. 11:4). He will be treated with the same partisan kindness he has shown. God will not judge or condemn him; he will be absolved.

Passing naturally from lenient judgment and pardon to kindness in general, the final exhortation assures generous charity that it will have a superabundant and permanent reward: "Give and you will receive; a goodly measure —pressed down, shaken together, running over—will be poured into your lap. The measure you use in measuring will be used to measure out your share" (v. 38). The Greek reads literally, "*They* will give you. . . ." "They" refers, of course, to God or to his angels (cf. 12:20, 48) but is intentionally left indefinite because the accent of the passage is on the size and permanence of the gift. All the qualities of charity prescribed by Jesus —patience, generosity, mercy, spontaneous sympathy for one's neighbor—amount in the final analysis to the total gift of goods and self. This demand is just as strict as the demand for exclusive service and consecration made by the love of God (Mt. 6:24). The comparison of the two precepts, which Jesus himself makes (Mt. 22:37, 39 and parallel accounts), shows that *agape* has an absolute hold on men and binds them over totally to God and neighbor.

## *Agape in the Gospel of St. Luke*

The implication is that the virtue is the same in both cases. That it refers radically to God seems normal enough, but that Jesus asked his disciples to consecrate themselves to their neighbor and even to their enemies in the same way may seem surprising. The secret of this equality is the disciples' elevation to the rank of God's sons; their morality could not be inferior to their dignity. A child is like his father, thinking as he does and imitating his gestures. Since God gives and pardons, his sons will be generous both with their possessions and with themselves.

The Christian will receive in his turn, for God's charity—measure of the disciple's charity—has no limit in giving (Jn. 3:34). The final sentence: "The measure you use in measuring will be used to measure out your share," —probably a current proverb—should not be understood as a mathematical reciprocity. It does not mean, "You will receive the equivalent of what you sacrificed; you will not lose anything; if you give little, you will get little; if you give much, you will get much." To let the disciple decide his own measure would be contrary to the Gospel. Really, there are only two measures possible, or, in other words, only two ways of reacting to this precept: to accomplish it or to refuse to accomplish it. If you give nothing, you will be given nothing, and no reward is the same as condemnation. If you are charitable, though, the good things you will receive will be entirely out of proportion with what you have given up (1 Cor. 2:9); half-measures are not considered.

The God whom Jesus puts before his disciples as their model will be himself the giver of their reward (Mt. 25:23). The morality of *agape*, the divine life lived on earth, has its fulfillment and support, its stability, in the heavenly reward. However disinterested in spirit they may be, God's sons still envisage and taste the eschatological joys of the harvest here below. The kingdom of God is already in their hearts. It is already theirs, and the Holy Spirit already inspires them and moves them to act. Through the Spirit they are authentic sons of God. Their sonship is the reason Jesus can prescribe a truly divine way of acting for them, even though he knows that no man can reach such an ideal. He merely wants his disciples to tend toward it. The Spirit he sends them reminds them always of their goal and urges them to draw closer and closer to it.

### THE CENTURION'S ESTEEM FOR THE JEWISH NATION

"He is *fond (agapan) of* our nation" (Lk. 7:5).

As soon as he had finished the Sermon on the Mount, Jesus went down to Capharnaum. There a pagan centurion, a Roman perhaps, confronted him with a slave who was critically ill. The parallel account in Matthew 8:6 explains that the servant was paralysed and in great pain, but Luke, usually so careful to make a diagnosis, emphasizes the psychological aspect instead. The master was very attached to his slave: "He thought very highly of him" (*entimos*) (v. 2). The Greek word was often used to describe "valuable things." Taken in this sense, the sentence would mean that the centurion, overwhelmed at the thought of losing a "valuable" servant whose help he needed, looked to the Lord for the cure that would restore him the services of this justly esteemed domestic.

## Agape in the Gospel of St. Luke

But for Luke to use this epithet of the market with the word "slave," thus implying that a slave was just a "thing," would have been deeply offensive to his Greek readers. *Entimos* should be given the meaning it usually has when applied to a person—"considered, esteemed, honored." It refers, not to the centurion's utilitarian interest in his slave, but to his esteem and real affection for him: "[His servant] was dear to him." Such humane feeling was so rare at the time that St. Luke makes a point of stressing the officer's nobility of heart. He was a soldier and a man of sensitivity.

The elders, that is, the members and perhaps the representatives, of the Jewish community of Capharnaum willingly interceded for the centurion with Jesus. They came with the urgent request that he save the sick man (v. 3). Their description of the pagan officer was more than favorable; it was a real encomium and was strongly presented: "He is the right man for you to grant him this favor. He is, certainly, *fond (agapan) of* our nation and has built the synagogue for us at his own expense" (vv. 4–5).

This is the first use of *agapan* in its profane sense in the New Testament. Luke chose the word to translate the expression used by the Jewish Galilean elders; it repeats the sense of the corresponding Hebrew word in the Old Testament and the Greek in the Septuagint. Its meaning is perfectly plain; the centurion's love was a clear-sighted affection for the Jewish nation. He was very well disposed toward the Israel he knew so deeply. He respected and even admired its monotheistic faith and proved his esteem by contributing substantially to the construction of the synagogue at Capharnaum.

*Agape in the New Testament*

The centurion was evidently a man of generous heart and of noble spirit. He was fond of his slave. He had won the admiration of a foreign people; he had faithful friends among them who shared his grief. His sensitivity to religious values had moved him to show his respect for the purity and transcendence of the Jewish religion. There was no greediness in him; he gave lavishly of his own wealth. Just as Jesus was moved by love for the rich young man, who was so faithful to God's commandments (Mk. 10:21), so also "on hearing [about the delicate and generous kindness of this pagan], Jesus was struck with admiration for him" (v. 9).

Since St. Luke took advantage of every opportunity to bring *agape*'s excellence into relief, it would not be rash to see here a desire to relate this episode to the Sermon on the Mount by choosing *agapan* as the verb in "he is fond of our nation," and by describing the centurion so movingly.[8] Luke shows that Jesus, acting like God himself, was the first to treat the Gentiles kindly and generously. He loved to emphasize that the Gentiles are called, just as are the Jews, to participate in the blessings of the kingdom. The officer is an image of the pagan's faith. This stranger's natural goodness formed a contrast to the rivalries and enmities that boiled up constantly in Israel. It enabled him to believe instinctively and immediately in the Savior's goodness. Grace builds on nature! "I have not found such lively faith even in Israel" (v. 10).

---

[8] "After he had completed his instructions in the hearing of the people, he visited Capharnaum" (Lk. 7:1) is both the historical conclusion to the Sermon and the introduction to the story of the cure of the centurion's servant.

## THE CHARITY OF THE SINFUL WOMAN, LK. 7:42, 47

One day, one of the Pharisees invited [Jesus] to a meal with him. He entered the home of the Pharisee and reclined on a couch; and without warning a woman who was a scandal in the town came in. After making sure that he was at table in the home of the Pharisee, she brought with her an alabaster flask of perfume, took her stand behind him at his feet, and wept. Yielding to an impulse, she rained her tears on his feet and wiped them with her hair; she tenderly kissed his feet and anointed them with the perfume. His host, the Pharisee, noticed this, and said to himself: "This man, if he were a prophet, would know who and what sort of creature this woman is, that makes so much fuss over him! Why, she is a scandalous person."

Jesus read his thoughts and said to him: "Simon, I have something to tell you." "Tell it, Rabbi," he replied. "Once upon a time two men were in the debt of a money lender. The one owed him five hundred denarii; the other, fifty. *Neither of them was in a position to pay; so he made both of them happy by canceling their debts. Under these circumstances, which of them will be more generous in loving* [agapan] *him?*" (v. 42). "The one, I suppose," answered Simon, "whom he made happy by canceling the greater amount." "Your judgment is correct," he replied. Then, turning to the woman, he said to Simon: "Do you see this woman? I came into your house, and you offered me no water for my feet: but this woman rained her tears upon my feet and wiped them dry with her hair. You gave me no kiss of welcome; but this woman has not left off, from the time I entered, tenderly kissing my feet. You did not anoint my head with oil: but this woman anointed my feet with perfume. *And in consideration of this I tell you: her sins, numerous as they are, are forgiven. You see, she has shown so much love* [agapan]. *One, of course, who has but little for-*

## Agape in the New Testament

*given him shows but little love* [agapan]" (v. 47). He then said to her: "Your sins are forgiven." At once his fellow guests gave way to thoughts like this: "Who is this individual who even forgives sins!" He finally said to the woman: "Your faith has saved you. Go home and be at peace" (Lk. 36–50).

The meaning of *agapan* (to love), used three times, depends closely upon the context. This incident is an example, not of Jesus' kindness to virtuous men like the centurion of Capharnaum (Lk. 7:1–10), but of his mercy to a notoriously sinful woman. Jesus was known for his goodness to publicans and to men of no reputation (v. 34). His universal charity did not stop with them, however, but included everyone; he formed relationships with the higher classes also and with men of recognized virtue, like the Pharisee whose invitation to dinner he had accepted.[4]

As soon as Jesus arrived at Simon's house, he took his place at the table. He lay on a slightly raised couch covered with rugs and cushions, supporting himself on his left elbow. He had removed his sandals (Jn. 1:27), and his bare feet faced the free area where the servants came and went.

---

[4] Cf. 11:37; 14:1. Simon the Pharisee seems to have been more curious about Jesus than friendly toward him. He invited him to dinner to watch him and find out more about him, not to honor him. Perhaps it was because Jesus understood his motives that he did not immediately accept the invitation. The imperfect tense of the Greek verb "invited," showing continuous action, suggests that the Pharisee insisted that he dine with him. As a matter of fact, the Pharisee acted very reserved toward Jesus, and his welcome was cold. As soon as Jesus came into the house, they began to dine, without any preliminary conversation or any of the usual ceremonies of hospitality which Jesus later mentions.

## Agape in the Gospel of St. Luke

The first words of verse 37 express great surprise. A woman appeared, and what a woman! She was a notorious sinner. The whole town knew her disreputable life. That is not to say she was a prostitute. If she were "the servants would not have allowed her to enter. There was a distinction about her that would have been impossible to such a woman, even repentent" (M. J. Lagrange, *Evangile selon saint Luc*³, Paris, 1927, *in h.v.*). She was a woman of good society, who had lived loosely. She had been involved in affair after affair, and she had nothing more to lose as far as reputation went. Only her rank in society guaranteed her a certain appearance of respect, and no one dared to forbid her entrance into the dining room.

The woman, who had lost all honor, wanted to honor Jesus as a distinguished person in a way customary in the East.⁵ She had brought a bottle of perfumed oil with her; the usual thing would have been to anoint Jesus' head. That she planned to pour the oil over his feet instead shows her deep awareness of her unworthiness. This awareness, joined to her desire to honor Jesus, reveals at once the quality of this woman in whom discretion and fervor were united. She made the depth of her veneration plain by her self-abasement and by the avowal of her own misery. She moved behind the table to the place where Jesus was reclining, and knelt down.

⁵ Such women do not care what people say, and sometimes even speak and act in order to provoke scorn from the respectable. Nevertheless, it was deeply humiliating for her to approach one whom she considered at least a prophet. It must have cost her dearly. But how or when could she hope to find another occassion to approach Jesus and reveal her feelings? "Love forced her not to wait for a more propitious occasion" (Bengel).

*Agape in the New Testament*

Suddenly something she had not in the least planned happened. She burst into tears [6] and wept and wept until Jesus' feet were thoroughly wet with her tears.

This "inundation" was most incorrect. To add to her emotion, the woman must have noticed at once a detail of courtesy; no one had washed Jesus' feet when he came into the house. They were still covered with that fine, flour-like dust that lies over the roads of Palestine. Nothing infuriates a woman more than to see the one she loves and respects treated shabbily. The sinful woman improvised a beautiful gesture. Instead of using her veil, her wide sleeves, or the hem of her cloak to wipe Jesus' feet, she undid her coiffure—an act singularly humiliating in public—and wiped his feet with her hair. Only the heart of a woman could have found so sweet an expression of her sorrowing love. Then, her first gesture calling forth another, she began to kiss the feet of her Lord over and over. The Greek verb used changes tense here to show that she held his feet and kissed them again and again. St. Luke arranged the scene to suggest the thoughts and feelings of the participants; for him her gesture was the high point of the scene. It revealed the woman's faith, her profound reverence for her Lord, her humility, affection, and love. Then she returned to her first purpose in coming and anointed his feet.

None of the speechless spectators dared make the slightest remark, but the "separated" Pharisee, to whom

---

[6] It would be impossible not to be reminded here of the beatitude of those who weep (Lk. 6:21). This sinful woman of Galilee may have heard some echo of the Sermon on the Mount. At any rate, her tears were surely tears of repentence and shame.

virtue was an aspect of legal purity, could not help being shocked. He decided that Jesus was not a prophet, as many supposed (Mk. 6:15). If he were, he would have known who this woman was and would not have let her treat him as she had. He would never have let her touch him.[7] Still, Simon, motionless and correct to the very end, did not budge and let her continue with her anointing (v. 39).

He was to have immediate proof that Jesus had the prophetic gift of reading the human heart. The Lord politely asked his host's permission to speak, and Simon coolly gave it to him. Jesus then presented him with a very uncomplicated hypothetical case. Two men both owed another man some money, one 500 denarii, the other 50. Although one owed much more than the other, both had the same problem. They could not pay their debts, which, it would seem, had fallen due. Their creditor had a legal means of recovering his money. He could have gone before the magistrate (Lk. 12:58), had his insolvent debtors arrested, their wages attached and their possessions sold, and even could have had them, their wives, and their children bound over to work for him as slaves. Obviously a creditor who was dubious about

[7] The Greek verb means more than "to touch" or "to make contact"; it can mean "to give oneself to." Simon was already indignant because the sinful woman touched Jesus, but more indignant still because she dared to approach him and enter into relationship with him. She "attacked" this Rabbi and prophet! Her act was both morally and physically incongruous. One Rabbi had taught that a distance of two and a half feet was to be kept from a courtesan. But as St. Albert the Great observes: "When the sinful woman touched the Holy of Holies, his sanctity was not desecrated but rather her sin cleansed" (*In Ev. Lucae*, in *h.v.*).

recovering his loan would prefer having the free services of his debtors to keeping them idle in prison. Or a creditor with a distaste for legal procedures might cancel part of his loan. He would get back some of his money and would have forced an acknowledgment of his rights. The creditor of the parable, however, like the master of the unfaithful steward (Lk. 16:1–2), seems remarkably detached from wealth and uninterested in law suits. His debtors were insolvent, but instead of taking them to court, he renounced his claim and dissolved the debts. This purely gratuitous act of kindness and generosity was just the opposite of what justice demanded. The moneylender's goodness reached out to the very persons of the debtors. He was thinking of other human beings, not of his rights or of his money. Their future relations were already determined by his magnificent generosity.

The point of the parable is, "Which of them will be more generous in loving him?" Judging from the context, *agapan* does not have the meaning, at least directly, of attachment, fidelity, or even esteem, but of grateful love, as it often does in classical Greek. Jesus asked Simon what each of the debtors should feel in the face of the amazing good will of the lender. We would say, "Which man will feel more gratitude?" Though there was no word "gratitude" in Hebrew or Aramean, *agapan* was especially apt for expressing the idea. It implied an affection very aware of its motive and easily aroused by a favor or kindness. In profane and Septuagint Greek, too, *agapan* expressed the return of love to a warm and generous benefactor. *Agapan*'s gratitude is active; it normally blossoms into acclaim and tries to

## Agape in the Gospel of St. Luke

make a return in service and care, to give signs of its loyalty, and to "acknowledge" the gift received.

It was so evident that the lender's attentive good will would arouse a proportionate response of *agape* in the debtor that Simon seemed annoyed at having to answer so simple a question. He spoke with lofty indifference and a certain scorn: "I suppose the one whom he made happy by canceling the greater amount." Jesus' straightforward approval of his answer was not without irony: "Your judgment is correct." Until then the Lord does not seem to have paid any attention to the woman, but he now turned toward her to point her out.[8] He mentioned the details of the homage he had received from her and contrasted them with Simon's neglect. It was not the just Pharisee who honored him but the despised, guilty woman. The carefully drawn contrast shows that Jesus identified the two debtors with the sinful woman and with Simon. The generous creditor was Jesus himself or God the Father. The two debtors have different attitudes. One is indifferent and cold; the other is eager to show respect, honor, and veneration. The last sentence adds that the woman's gestures were an expression of her fervent love: "In consideration of this I tell you: her sins, numerous as they are, are forgiven. You see, *she has shown so much love*." These verbs in the present tense can be applied generally as well as to the sinful woman and Simon. *Agapan* denotes a manifest love, an attachment that expresses and proves itself. In verse 42 *agapan* had the direct object "him": "Which of

---

[8] Jesus' question to Simon: "Do you see this woman?" probably had the tone of an order or of an invitation to meditate on what she had done as well as to look at her.

## Agape in the New Testament

them will be more generous in loving him?" Here it is used without an object; consequently its exact meaning has to be determined by the context. *Agapan* might be a love of affection properly speaking, that is, of dilection. To avoid any equivocation our Lord discreetly refrained from being more explicit about the intensity of the woman's sentiments. They were, after all, addressed as much to the Father of mercy as to himself. In her case *agapan* would keep the religious meaning of adoration and choice it had in the Septuagint. The word can also mean "to desire, to long for" and express the woman's urgent longing for purification and for pardon. The "absolution" at last accorded her seems a confirmation and response to her deepest desire. The sentiments which brought about the repentant woman's return to God were many and complex; therefore, none of these nuances of *agapan* should be excluded. The obvious interpretation of the woman's acts, especially for an inhabitant of the Near East, was as homage. The sentence, "She has shown so much love," should be understood as a reference to the preceding scene. This is the meaning the first commentators gave it: "She has shown so much honor, veneration, and respect." The perfume, kisses, and tears were the expression of her faith, confidence, humility, fear, and love.

*Agapan*'s meaning in this passage is clear now. It is harder to determine the relation between love and pardon. "In consideration of this, I tell you: her sins, numerous as they are, are forgiven. You see, she has shown so much love." According to the logic of the situation it would seem at first reading that Jesus took the woman's gestures for manifestations of love and was saying that "charity" won the remission of her sins and merited her pardon. This is the interpretation of the Vulgate, the Fathers, and many modern exegetes. However, the unity of the passage demands that verse 47 be interpreted according to the parable of the two acquitted debtors. It could then be translated, "Henceforth she will love much because much had been forgiven her"; or, "Numerous sins must have been forgiven her since she has shown such love." In this case, love would be the effect and not the cause of the pardon.

This interpretation has two advantages. It retains one meaning, love of gratitude, for all the uses of *agapan* in the passage. It also brings the two apparently disparate sentences into harmony. Many exegetes have adopted it and have tried to justify their translations by theories that are unfortunately more ingenious than reasonable. Their error is in not accepting a text unanimously upheld by the manuscripts and in trying to reduce a situation vibrant with complex emotions to a rigid simplicity. It is true that the first part of verse 47 is not in harmony with the parable. The second part, "one who has but little forgiven him shows but little love [to his benefactor]" is an exact application. Our Lord was thinking of Simon, in whom a salutary uneasiness must have arisen as he identified himself with the debtor who had the least forgiven. As often happens, the parable had turned into an allegory. Jesus had proposed a concrete example designed to awaken Simon's conscience; then he continued the conversation and suggested, from the differing attitudes of Simon and of the woman, the contrast between the feeling of the just and of sinners toward him. He concluded with two sentences. The first applied specifically to the woman, and the second, although directed primarily toward Simon, remained general and impersonal. From the difference in the persons addressed and from the formulation of the sentences, we may conclude that each had its distinct meaning.

Simon has little forgiven him, but he is among those who think themselves virtuous (Lk. 18:9)—Pharisees and anonymous small debtors, mentioned here for contrast and because Jesus happened to be in the house of one of them. For them Jesus was content to apply the parable strictly. They were faithful observers of the Law with little to be pardoned for. They would love only a little and that with a love of gratitude, making the return due in the "justice" they understood so well.

The entire narrative, however, centers around the sinful woman, and it was to her that Jesus spoke first. She would surely show immense gratitude in the future, since the Lord was about to absolve her many sins. In her touching tenderness and fervor Jesus had recognized a loving and religious soul. Without speaking a word, this woman had shouted her adoration, her attachment to him, her desire of purification, and her will to be faithful—all manifestations in the Old Covenant of authentic *agape*. Jesus was deeply moved by her just as he had been by the rich young man who desired to be perfect, the good and generous centurion, and the Samaritan woman who had so delicate a perception of spiritual realities. To conclude the secret dialogue between his soul and hers, he introduced a new thought, one not directly connected with the parable.

The explanation for the lack of an apparent link between the first part of verse 47 and the parable of the

## Agape in the Gospel of St. Luke

debtors is in the evolving situation, the prolonged conversation, and the operations of grace, which have nothing to do with the logic of literary genres. The mistake of many exegetes has been to see this passage simply as the portrait of a sinful woman pardoned and then likened to a debtor. In fact, it describes a living scene that puts three persons in relationship with one another. It should be called, "Jesus, the Pharisee, and the sinful woman." Here is the way we understand it.

In his heart Simon proudly and disdainfully condemned the woman who had prostrated herself at Jesus' feet. "Able to tell what was in a man" (Jn. 2:24), Jesus knew perfectly well that she had committed many sins. He also knew that she was truly penitent; hence, he invited the Pharisee to discover what her actions meant. She had showed her love in the form of religious veneration. He, the object of her faith and adoration, responded by pardoning her. The lesson here is not only that love can obtain the remission of sins,[9] but also that great sinners are usually the most sincere in their contrition and charity: *peccata multa . . . dilexit multum*. It should not be surprising that God takes their sincerity into account and absolves them from their immense debt (Mt. 21:31). The parable's teaching is to the point. It reveals that God, a good creditor, pardons graciously; the person in debt, attractive or not, is always capable of loving—and it is love that saves.

The repentant sinner's *agape* will certainly be differ-

---

[9] A. Nygren is incorrect when he asserts: "There is no way going from men to God, only a way from God to man, *agape*" (*Eros und Agapè*, Gütersloh, 1930). The love of the sinful woman proves what was already clear in the Septuagint, that *agape* can ascend from man to God.

## Agape in the New Testament

ent before and after his justification. Love for the person of Christ can win pardon, but once the soul is purified, pardon brings an increase of love in deep gratitude. *Agape* has many nuances and intensities. "Which will love him most?" (v. 42); "she has shown *so much* love" (v. 47ᵃ); "he shows *but little* love" (v. 47ᵇ). The lesson of the passage could be called "Of Great and Small Love of God." The parable of the sower makes the fecundity of God's word depend on the receptivity of the soil, thus explaining the overwhelming differences in man's love and worship of God and of Christ. St. John says: "An evildoer hates the light . . . but one who lives up to the truth comes to the light" (Jn. 3:20–21). St. Luke shows that "public" sinners (Lk. 7:34), known to everyone as worthless, great debtors that they are, feel more love and desire and gratitude than the haloed virtuous. Their *agape* gives them first title to enter into the New Covenant. This is the great revelation of the Gospel of mercy.

Neither the woman nor Jesus had spoken to each other. His first words to her were surely said with great tenderness in his voice and expression: "Your sins are forgiven" (v. 48). The form of the verb in Greek shows that the debt was remitted at that moment and would remain so (cf. v. 20). The fact that the woman loved before she was acquitted is thus confirmed.

The onlookers were scandalized that Jesus would arrogate to himself the right to make such a decision (v. 49; cf. Mt. 9:1–6). Aware of their unbelief, Jesus added: "Your faith has saved you. Go home and be at peace" (v. 50). Many commentators are amazed that her salvation, at first attributed to her charity, is now made to depend on her faith. Others take these words as a stereotyped formula routinely used to conclude miracles and without any particular meaning here. Actually, they fit the situation perfectly. They were directed toward the onlookers, whose incredulity Luke had just mentioned. In contrast to the petty, distrustful, unloving debtors, the great faith of this great sinner made her able to receive all the gifts of salvation, so much more vast than forgiveness of sin. The assurance of salvation may be considered a promise to her of new gifts. Besides, faith itself is a more ample reality than the *agape* it arouses and includes (Gal. 5:6). Our Lord knew that faith had led the woman to him and had humiliated her before him. He cherished her faith and rewarded it with salvation. The woman had known he was the Messias or someone divine. She was sure he represented God and that he loved sinners (Lk. 7:34). She trusted him as an accessible and generous creditor (v. 42) who was able to remit sins (Lk. 5:17–26). Her belief was more than a conviction of mind and an intuition of heart. She adhered to the Lord in love and in religious adoration, expressing herself in the spontaneous overflow of *agape*. What saved her and won her pardon was her *obsequium fidei*—the offering of her faith (Phil. 2:17)—her worship of the true God in sacrifice, submission (2 Cor. 10:5), and the total gift of self (Rom. 12:1; cf. 9:4; Jn. 16:2). The reading of *agapan* in verse 47 as a love of religion and of worship is, therefore, correct. The woman adored her Lord, offering him her entire life.

Her surrender to love and to gratitude were plain to be seen in her expression. Jesus suggested that she withdraw from the room, which was filled with hostile onlookers. Go in peace, in the peace of heart which you will keep always. Taking her treasure with her, she disappeared.

## CHARITY PRESCRIBED FOR THE SCRIBE AND ACCOMPLISHED BY THE SAMARITAN

"*Love* the Lord your God with your whole heart, and with your whole soul, and with your whole strength, and with your whole mind, and *love* your neighbor as yourself" (Lk. 10:27).

This pericope parallels Matthew 22:34-40 and Mark 12:28-34, which have already been analyzed (cf. *supra* pp. 26-32; 62-66). A lawyer had put a test question to Jesus; he asked him what he should do to obtain eternal life. Jesus had him recite the commandments of the Law as a child would do. The Scribe felt ridiculous and thought that he had asked too simple a question. "Anxious to justify it" and show himself no simple man, he immediately asked: "And who is my neighbor?" (v. 29). Jesus answered him by relating the parable of the Good Samaritan.

A man was travelling along a deserted road. He was no one in particular; neither his race, nationality, religion, nor any of his circumstances are described. He fell in with robbers who stripped and beat him and left him lying on the road. A priest and a Levite passed by, one after the other, but both avoided the place where he was lying, apparently not bothering even to glance in his direction. Next a Samaritan came along. He stopped and took care of the wounded man and then brought him to a safe place. Our Lord ended his story with a

## Agape in the Gospel of St. Luke

question of his own: "Which of these three men seems to you to have been neighbor to the man who had fallen in with the bandits?" (v. 36).

At first glance, Jesus' question does not seem to correspond to the Scribe's, "Who is my neighbor?" He had probably meant, "Who precisely is the object of the 'charity' prescribed by the Law—is it a compatriot, a proselyte, a pagan? Toward whom am I bound to observe this precept?" However Jesus answered the question, the Scribe planned to object, in the name either of the Law or of oral tradition; under certain conditions one should ignore and refuse to help the impure, the idolatrous. Not only did Jesus refuse to answer him with a definition of "neighbor," but in his parable and final question he set up a new problem: How does one act as "neighbor"? Which of the three passers-by behaved as a neighbor by joining the unknown victim to help him?

Because Jesus' parable introduces this new question, many critics believe the dialogue with the Scribe (vv. 25–28) originally formed a document separate from that of the parable (vv. 30–37). According to this theory, St. Luke used the dialogue as an introduction to the parable, joining them artificially by the question: "Who is my neighbor?" (v. 29). Others have noticed that the parable responds essentially to the question; a neighbor is every man who is in need. That is true, but it is not what Jesus' last question asks. "Which of the travellers showed himself a neighbor to the man in need?"

The apparent contradiction disappears with less attention to the words and more to the living reality of the situation. Rigid logic in Occidental style will not serve in dealing with Oriental mentality, which loves enigmas, parables, and proverbs. Precise definition of a word or of a notion is no help. It is necessary to perceive what an image suggests and to respond to unspoken questions.

To begin with, the "parable" of the Samaritan is not, strictly speaking, a comparison, much less an argument designed to persuade. It is rather a paradigm, a pattern story, a concrete, particular case illustrating a point of doctrine and presenting a model to be imitated.[10] The Scribe had come, perhaps in good faith, perhaps not, to ask what *he* must do to have eternal life. Humiliated at having been forced to answer his own question, he tried to involve Jesus in a scholarly debate and escape his embarrassment on the speculative plane. But the Lord, always master of the situation, turned the discussion as he wished it to go. He had been taking the Scribe's questions seriously and directing his answers toward the salvation of souls. He had used the occasion of the sinful woman's pardon to awaken in Simon an appreciation of the love of gratitude. Now he refused a technical definition in order to give the light of life instead. What is important is not *knowing* who is a neighbor, but *acting* with charity to all men, whoever they may be. Both the parable and Jesus' last question are clear answers to the Scribe's, "What must I do to obtain a place in eternal life?"

It is not even certain that the Scribe's second question,

[10] Cf. J. M. Creed, *The Gospel according to St. Luke* (London, 1953), p. 150. These *exempla* are peculiar to Luke: cf. the foolish rich man (12:16–21); the rich man and the beggar Lazarus (16:19–31); the Pharisee and the publican (18:10–14); and the two debtors (7:40–42).

## Agape in the Gospel of St. Luke

as it is phrased in Greek, means exactly: "Who is my neighbor?" or even that it had only one meaning for the doctor of the Law. The Greek text has the adverb "neighborly" without the article preceding as it had in verse 27 ("Love your neighbor"). This difference in formulation suggests a difference in meaning. If we understand: "Who is neighbor to me?" or "Who, exactly, is a neighbor to me?" the parable becomes a perfect answer to this moral problem about a practical action. The Samaritan alone both felt and behaved as a neighbor to the wounded man; charity, then, makes of a stranger a neighbor. By love we become brothers of all men, whether or not they are already close to us by blood, nationality, religion, or any other bond. The dialogue had been extremely rapid. The Scribe had put his question vigorously: "And who is my neighbor?" The Lord did not let him continue, either because he guessed that a trap was coming or because he wanted to use the occasion to present a new teaching. He seems to have interrupted the Scribe in picking up his last word, "neighbor." The Greek words translated, "Jesus replied" (v. 30), may also mean "Jesus picked up again" the thought of the dialogue. He returned to its original point. To obtain eternal life one must . . . "love his neighbor as himself" (v. 27). The Scribe wanted to clarify the notion of "neighbor"; Jesus explained "love," as he had already done in the Sermon on the Mount. Prophet of the New Covenant, he defined with authority the meaning of the *agape* prescribed by God. The Scribe did not object that his question had not been answered. That he acquiesced in the Lord's teaching shows that the fundamental question really concerned *agape* and that "neighbor" can be defined only in terms of living love and not according to juridical categories.

It must be recognized, then, not only that the story of Luke 10:25–37 is homogeneous but also that it is one of the Gospel's richest teachings on the love of charity. Our Lord invited the Scribe to reflect: "Which of these three men seems to you to have been neighbor to the man who had fallen in with the bandits?" (v. 36). The question concerned all three men who traveled that road, not just the Samaritan. The priest and the Levite represented the hierarchy, the quintessence of Judaism. They were included to signify the opposition between the letter of the Old Covenant and the spirit of the New. They may have had excellent reasons for avoiding the wounded man. Perhaps there were conditions that justified their refusal to help someone in danger. The man lying in the road was unknown to them and probably could not even be identified. His misfortune might have been a divine punishment which should not be interfered with. If they went near him, they might contract legal defilement and become incapable of carrying out the ritual ceremonies: "Whoever touches the dead body of any human being shall be unclean for seven days; . . . moreover, everyone who in the open country touches a dead person, whether he was slain by the sword or died naturally, or who touches a human bone or a grave, shall be unclean for seven days" (Nm. 19:11, 14). Admittedly, their attitudes suggested total indifference more than concern for legal purity, and it is remarkable indeed that the Lord has not one word of blame for them. Jesus practiced the charity he preached; his all-demanding *agape* had nothing sectarian or aggressive in it.

*Agape in the Gospel of St. Luke*

The hero of the parable is a Samaritan, a man from whom generosity would never be expected. It is important to remember how the very word "Samaritan" sounded to contemporary ears. Its history began with Sargon's capture of Samaria in 722 B.C. The Assyrian monarch massacred part of the population and deported the surviving Samaritan men. He repopulated the country with emigrant Arabs, Babylonians, and others. The newcomers intermarried with the remaining Samaritans. Although they admitted Yahweh to their pantheon, they also kept the cult of their own divinities. The ethnic mixture led to the greatest confusion in religion. When the Jews returned from the Babylonian captivity, the Samaritans, who claimed to be followers of Yahweh, made an official offer to Zorobabel and Joshua to assist in the reconstruction of the Temple. Their offer was refused because they did not belong to the holy nation (Esd. 4:3). Afterwards, hostility between the two groups grew stronger. The Samaritans raised up "the people of the country" against the project of reconstruction and denounced it to Artaxerxes (vv. 4–16). Under Alexander the Great—who sent them a group of Macedonian colonists—they took in turncoat priests from Jerusalem and every malcontent who decided to leave the Israelite community. They erected a schismatic temple on Gerizim, "the blessed mountain," and rejected the prophets, keeping only the Pentateuch as inspired Scripture. The best Jerusalemites considered this motley group of emigrants and half-breeds perfect specimens of traitors and apostates. "My whole being loathes two nations, the third is not even a people: Those who live in Seir and Philistia, and the degenerate folk who dwell in Shichem"

(Sir. 50:25–26). At the time of the Machabees the Samaritans made common cause with the invaders against the Jews. They went so far as to write to King Antiochus congratulating him for treating the Jews "as their wickedness deserved." They joined themselves entirely to his cause, even to the extent of designating their temple of Gerizim as the temple of Zeus and considering the Sabbath observance a superstitious practice.

For a Jew of the first century A.D., a Samaritan was a stereotype of stranger, enemy, and heretic. Racial, political, and religious antagonisms had gradually developed into absolute contempt. It is understandable that the synagogue considered the Samaritans impure and forbade them access to the Temple. Their religious contributions were refused and their testimony was not accepted in courts of justice. Not only was marriage with a Samaritan woman forbidden, but also accepting food or drink from one of them was against the Law. The Samaritans were equally hostile to the Jews. If anyone so much as intended to go to Jerusalem, the Samaritan refused him all hospitality. This was the reason the Sons of Thunder wanted to call down fire from heaven upon these impious people (Lk. 9:52, 54).

Our Lord's choosing a Samaritan to play the hero's role in his parable on fraternal love is significant. This heretical stranger, without the learning of the Scribe and without the religious dignity of the priest and of the Levite, showed himself profoundly human and profoundly religious. He put the two great commandments of the Old Testament into practice in the spirit of the New Covenant. Of the three travelers, he was the true Israelite. In the Sermon on the Mount, Jesus had asked

## Agape in the Gospel of St. Luke

his disciples not to limit their love to those near them who had already shown them affection. Christians were to distinguish themselves from sinners by becoming or by showing themselves sons of the Most High in the enormous reach of their charity (Lk. 6:32–34). Here, however, the model of authentic *agape* is a Samaritan who helped a man he knew nothing about. Does this not mean that true children of God existed outside official religion and that Jesus had come to gather them all together (Jn. 11:52)? A Samaritan woman had received the revelation that real worshippers, regardless of race and of ritual, are those who worship the Father in spirit and in truth (Jn. 4:23–24). Surely charity constitutes the worship that is agreeable to the Father. The parable teaches for the first time that charity obtains eternal life (vv. 25, 28, 37), as St. Paul and St. John later emphasize so forcefully.

The Samaritan's conduct revealed a perfect charity and enriched the concept of *agapan* enormously. Love is characterized by its *spontaneity* and *promptness*. The Scribe knew the precept of love of neighbor and wanted to find out how far it extended. He was not willing to love unless he had to and then he would love only in the required degree. The Samaritan loved without even thinking of the Law or trying to find out who the object of his care was. His goodness welled up spontaneously, as God's does, who cherishes his creatures independently of their lovableness.

In the Sermon on the Mount our Lord had asked that love be larger than mere response to affection already received. Not only was the Samaritan the first to love, but also he loved *disinterestedly;* his charity was pure gift. Consequently, the notion of "neighbor" as someone with whom there was an already-existing relationship, a greater or lesser "proximity," disappears. The question is no longer one of finding among all humanity the persons we can love, but of loving, purely and simply, whether or not the others are lovable.

The Samaritan's charity, in marked contrast to his predecessors' indifference, was singularly *personal, active,* and *effective*. He interrupted his trip, bandaged the man's wounds, and took care of his expenses. He did these things personally. Great as his generosity with his money was, it did not begin to match the value of his personal involvement. His love aroused in him a profound interest in the misery of the wounded man, and he reached out to him directly and personally.

The supreme revelation of the parable of the good Samaritan is that charity is composed of *compassion* and *mercy*. It was already known to be a love of adoration and of gratitude toward God, strong enough to dominate all bitterness and anger; one was to pray for enemies and even show them respect and help them. A centurion, like the one from Capharnaum, proved his love for strangers by his benefactions. The Samaritan must have suspected that the wounded man lying on the road between Jerusalem and Jericho would be a Jew, a detested enemy. Yet he not only helped him but also was deeply moved at seeing him so badly treated. Our Lord stressed this response; as soon as the Samaritan saw the wounded man, he was moved to pity (v. 33). The verb in Greek conveys a great deal. It is proper to the synoptic writers, who use it only when speaking of Christ. Compassion is

## Agape in the Gospel of St. Luke

a feeling profoundly suited to the Savior. It is a physical emotion experienced in the face of grief, pain, or misery in others. Jesus never resisted it; it explains his miracles. St. Luke accounts for it as being the result of an encounter with grief; faced with great sorrow, Jesus is filled with pity. When he was approaching the town of Naim he met the funeral "of a dead man [who] was the only son of his widowed mother," and "when he saw her his heart went out to her, and he said: 'Weep no more'" (Lk. 7:12, 13). He seems to remember his feeling and to attribute the same pity to the Samaritan, whose compassion sent him straight to the wounded man to take care of him. The priest and Levite were incapable of experiencing this pure and true compassion, but it explains everything the Samaritan did. And compassion is an integral part of charity.

The Scribe understood. He knew that to win eternal life he had to love his neighbor. Our Lord had given him a beautiful example of fraternal charity and then asked: "Which of these men seems to you to have been 'neighbor' to the wounded man?" (v. 36). The Scribe answered: "The one who showed him kindness" (v. 37). This equivalence of love of neighbor (v. 27) with kindness to him (v. 37) brings a note of tenderness to *agape* in the New Testament analagous to that given in the Old Testament by the spouse of the Canticle. Our Lord's approval: "Go and do as he did," shows this exegesis to be correct. A good heart, moved to pity by every man's sorrow, is charitable; it will live eternally.

Not the least wonderful fact about the scene is that the Samaritan, who acknowledged only the Pentateuch, applied the most elevated teaching of the prophets: "For it is love that I desire, not sacrifice, and knowledge of God rather than holocausts" (Os. 6:6).

## LOVE OF APPLAUSE AND OF BEING FIRST

"You are doomed, Pharisees! You *set great store* by front seats in synagogues and ceremonious greetings in public places" (Lk. 11:43).

Jesus excoriated the Scribes' and Pharisees' inflexible antagonism toward him in six curses condemning their greed, hypocrisy, and vanity: "You are doomed, Pharisees! You set great store by front seats in synagogues and ceremonious greetings in public places!" Vanity is universal. Pagans have surrendered to it (cf. Plutarch, *Banquet*, 1:2; Athenaeus, *Supper of the Sophists*, 2:8); the apostles paid it tribute in bickering about precedence (Mt. 20:20–28; Mk. 10:35–45; Lk. 22:24); and all Christians are in danger from it (Mk. 9:33–37; Lk. 14:7–11; Jas. 2:1–4). Jesus' enemies were shameless in their craving for honor. In the synagogues they tried to get the best places, those slightly elevated and facing the people, reserved for dignitaries, priests, elderly men, and doctors. Outside they lingered in the crowded market place to accept the deferential greetings they loved.

Ostentation was so characteristic of the Pharisees that St. Luke mentions it again in a later chapter: "Beware of the Scribes who *fancy* fine robes for outdoor wear and *crave* ceremonious greetings in public places and the front seats in the synagogue" (20:46). St. Matthew, too, records it: "They are *fond* of front seats in the synagogues; they *crave* ceremonious greetings in the public

## Agape in the Gospel of St. Luke

places" (23:6-7). St. Mark has: "Beware of the Scribes who *fancy* fine robes for outdoor wear, and ceremonious greeting in public places" (12:38-39).

Luke was the only writer to use *agapan* in this context. Comparison with the other texts suggests that it is a synonym of *philein*, the verb used in his second characterization of the Pharisees (20:46). This follows Matthew 23:6, which is the oldest text and Luke's inspiration. The immediate context of Luke 11:43 explains the unexpected use of *agapan* and calls for a slightly different nuance of *philein*. In the preceding curse, the Lord had condemned the Pharisees who paid tithes scrupulously and cared nothing for justice toward their neighbor or for love (*agape*) of God (v. 42). This is the only place St. Luke uses the noun *agape*, and it is understandable that he choose the corresponding verb for the next line. The thought moves along smoothly. Instead of trying to love God and then manifest that "love," the Pharisees "love" and seek honors and recognition. They savor the deliciousness of receiving homage from men when they ought to be concerned with giving homage to God. *Agapan* in Luke 11:43 has, then, its usual meaning in classical Greek, "to be content, satisfied, happy." [11]

This use of *agapan* in the profane sense is an index to the literary culture of St. Luke. He uses the verb with all the rich meaning a classical writer would give it. Sinners are *attached* to those who love them (6:32). The centurion acts according to his *esteem* for the Jewish

---

[11] *Prolégomènes*, pp. 40, 175 n. 3, 184 etc. The meaning is confirmed by its parallel construction with the verb *thelo* (Lk. 20:46; Mk. 12:38) which, when constructed with *en*, means, as it did in the Septuagint, "to take pleasure in, to be pleased with."

religion he *respects* so much (7:5). Debtors are *grateful* to their *liberal* creditor, and the sinful woman expresses her *veneration* for her Lord (7:42, 47). The Pharisees *show their preference* for their own glory and are completely happy when they are honored. Their egoism is radically opposed to the gift of self and the renouncement required by *agape* toward God.

### CHARITY, EXCLUSIVE CHOICE AND SERVICE OF GOD

"No servant can be the slave of two masters; for either he will hate the one and *love* the other . . ." (Lk. 16:13 = Mt. 6:24; cf. *supra*, p. 16 ff.

## The noun *agape*

### THE PRIMACY OF CHARITY TOWARD GOD

"You are doomed, Pharisees! You pay a ten per cent income tax on mint and rue and every garden herb, but disregard justice and the *love* [*agape*] of God" (Lk. 11:42).

This is the second use of the noun *agape* in the synoptic Gospels (cf. Mt. 24:12), and its only use with an object. Its infrequent appearance, when the verb is found so frequently, shows that the noun was absorbed much more slowly into Christian language. This slow absorption can be seen, too, in the "pessimistic" context in which *agape* appears in Matthew 24:12 and in Luke 11:42. In Matthew it is a virtue disappearing among Christians and in Luke a virtue lacking among the Pharisees. In Luke its meaning is necessarily one of those found in the Septuagint. What exactly is that meaning?

## Agape in the Gospel of St. Luke

The idea of the verse is clear. Our Lord was opposing the conduct he had just prescribed for his disciples to the practices of the Pharisees. These honorable gentlemen paid tithes on vegetables and neglected the great commandments. In the parallel text of Matthew 23:23, clearly more original, these "great" commandments are called weightier, more noble, and more important. Matthew lists them as "justice, mercy, and good faith"; Luke omits "good faith" entirely and substitutes "the love of God" for "mercy."

Matthew's "mercy" meant compassion or fraternal love. When Luke wrote "love" in place of "mercy," he certainly intended to evoke the precept of love, but by adding "of God" he corrected Matthew and showed that love of God and not love of neighbor was in question. There was no need, therefore, to mention "good faith," and, besides love, he included only justice. The word "justice" is used in its broadest sense to mean all right action, especially action involving the rights of others. According to the language of the Septuagint, "to mete out justice" is to act uprightly, especially when the proper conduct has been made explicit in a law. It would seem, then, that St. Luke's "justice and the love of God" refers to duties toward God and neighbor, as it did in 10:27, but in inverse order.

The meaning of *agape* here is clear: charity toward God—adoration, attachment, and fidelity—as in Deuteronomy. The Pharisees were scrupulous about observing infinitesimally detailed rules; Jesus opposed to their degenerate religion the true worship and service of God, where all care is for his glory. Tithing is a good thing, but when one concentrates his whole being on such exterior practices, he loses the sense of God's transcendence and is in danger of perverting his own sense of religion. *Agape* presupposes esteem, a recognition of God's excellence; it retains here its classical and spiritual meaning, "to value highly, to prefer." The Pharisees' narrow formalism had developed at the expense of the sovereign respect due God and had falsified the true hierarchy of religious values. Our Lord reproached his adversaries for not valuing adherence to God and concern for their neighbor above all else.

## The adjective *agapetos*

*Agapetos.* The Father declared his love for his son at the baptism (Lk. 3:22; cf. Mt. 3:17; Mk. 1:11) and Jesus declared himself beloved by God in the parable of the murderous vinedressers (Lk. 20:13; cf. Mk. 12:6). These texts have been analyzed *supra* pp. 37 ff.; 67 ff.

## Conclusion

Even at the first reading, Luke's language appears richer and more supple than Matthew's or Mark's. He uses *agapan* and *agape* in the many senses they had in profane and Septuagint Greek. The debtors were grateful to the creditor who canceled their debt (7:42). The Pharisees sought the first places and were happy in occupying them (11:43) instead of seeking God and preferring his honor to their own (11:42). The centurion respected the Jewish nation and admired the purity of its

## Agape in the Gospel of St. Luke

worship (7:5). Their affection for friends and benefactors made true lovers out of pagans and even sinners.

St. Luke agrees with Matthew and Mark in the doctrine that Christ alone is an adequate object of the Father's charity (3:22; 20:13). Using the same terms as St. Matthew, he stresses that the love of Christians for God is an adoration, implying religious consecration, exclusive choice, and fidelity (16:13). To love God with charity is the supreme obligation (10:27), although degrees are possible in this love (much, more, little, 7:42, 47) according as the lover realizes the gratuitousness and extent of God's gift. Man's love for God is fed by gratitude; he is a sinner who knows himself to be forever indebted for the remission of his faults. We may conclude that man's *agape*, fundamentally adoration and attachment, will acclaim the divine goodness in religious and grateful love, in exact fidelity, and in the service which is also worship.

St. Luke joins love of neighbor more closely to love of God than did Matthew and Mark (10:27). He sees the essence of the Sermon on the Mount in love of neighbor (6:27–38). Jesus' whole moral teaching is expressed in the one imperative: Love! Charity, which extends to the wicked, to enemies, to strangers, is strong enough to assure Christians perfect mastery over themselves and to direct all their action. By love the disciple of Christ can dominate his anger (6:29), remain patient under tribulation and spite (v. 27), and meet ill will with kindness and gentleness (vv. 29, 31). Love makes him speak well of his adversaries and instinctively show them respect (v. 28). In other words, his charity, expecting nothing in return for its kindness, is disinterestedly founded on total

## Agape in the New Testament

self-renouncement. One may strip himself of all he possesses, even down to his tunic. He may pay no attention to the reactions of his own self-love or of his wounded honor. He may be truly and generously kind to his enemy. Nevertheless, *agape* will have free rein only if his sacrifice of self is authentic and complete. *Agape* is a continuously-given gift (v. 30), always active and effective (vv. 27, 31, 33).

For St. Matthew, the disciple of Jesus Christ who loves this way becomes perfect as the heavenly Father is perfect. The God of St. Luke, however, is above all kind and compassionate (6:35–36; cf. Mt. 20:15; Mk. 10:18). He displays his perfection in his free and generous mercy to ungrateful and wicked men. Jesus himself was all compassion (7:13); hence, St. Luke introduces mercy as a constant element of *agape*. The good Samaritan, model of fraternal love, devoted himself personally and effectively to the wounded stranger he found on his path. His devotion arose from the deep pity he felt when he saw someone injured. The compassionate man truly suffers. He is stirred to the depths of his heart; he is physically moved. To say that this text of St. Luke marks a revolution in the semantics of *agapan* is no exaggeration. To love with charity meant in classical Greek to honor one's neighbor by showing him kindness or gratitude. In the religious language of the Septuagint, charity toward God was adoration, worship, obedience. This predilection resided in the highest and noblest faculties of man. Tenderness, rooted in man's emotions, was added now as a mark of *agape*. The Christian is no longer a reasonable man who appreciates another's good qualities and adjusts his own attitude accordingly, but a being made entirely of love, given body and soul to his neighbor, touched by whatever touches him. Forgetting himself completely, he will devote himself to others without even thinking of the cost. His love's compassion and effectiveness reveal his *agape* to be authentic—the *agape* of God, his Father: "Be compassionate as your Father is compassionate" (6:36).

The disciples of Jesus Christ are sons of the Most High (v. 35); this sonship is their nobility. It will be their title to an inconceivably great reward (v. 38). Loving God and neighbor is the means of obtaining eternal life (10:25), of sharing the very life of God in heaven.

CHAPTER IV

# Conclusion: Agape in the Synoptic Gospels

The synoptic Gospels never say expressly that God has *agape* for men. They do call him "good" and "compassionate" (Lk. 6:35, 36); his kindness is shown to be generous and universal. As a Father he knows and satisfies the disciples' needs (Mt. 6:8). He watches over the very hairs of their heads. The greatest of gifts, the Holy Spirit (Lk. 11:13), is his answer to their prayers. His goodness reaches to all people, wicked or good. It makes the lifegiving sun to shine and the rain to fall. The synoptic writers present God's lavish generosity as a model of the charity the disciples of Jesus must practice toward their neighbors, no matter how unpleasant or hostile.

Although he is all perfection, the God of the Gospels could not possibly be taken for a transcendent being, withdrawn into absolute and unapproachable solitude, isolated in a kind of Stoic insensibility. He has an only son whom he loves uniquely, whom he delights in calling his beloved (Mt. 3:17; Mk. 1:11; Lk. 3:22; Mt. 14:5; Mk. 9:7; cf. Mt. 12:8). Yet he did not hesitate to send his son to deal with the leaders of his people, although these leaders had stubbornly refused the message of his servants the prophets (Mk. 12:6; Lk. 20:13). God did not resign himself to breaking with men and punishing their revolts; instead he guided them to repentance. He submitted his son to insults and death. These men God loves so patiently and pursues so solicitously are characterized throughout the Gospels as wicked (Lk. 11:13), unjust (Mt. 5:45), and ungrateful (Lk. 6:35).

This amazing conception of God and of his relations with humanity is the first revelation of the Gospel—the

## Agape in the New Testament

revelation of a God who loves sinful men with charity. True, Yahweh had already shown his predilection for his people by mercifully intervening for them many times in history. Israel had betrayed his trust, however, and it would have been just for Israel to make the first move to ask his pardon. "Seek the Lord while he may be found, call him while he is near. Let the scoundrel forsake his way, and the wicked man his thoughts; let him turn to the Lord for mercy; to our God, who is generous in forgiving" (Is. 55:6–7). Men, sinners all, are debtors in the face of God, radically incapable of discharging their indebtedness (Lk. 7:41; cf. 11:4). God's goodness did not wait for them to make the first move toward repentance, but awoke their grief. The coming of the kingdom of heaven upon earth was precisely this appeal to repentance, this free invitation from God to guilty man to come to him and live in his company. God is a king who invites not only distinguished men to his son's wedding feast but also the poor, the crippled, the blind, and the lame. His son is a sower who casts the good seed of the word of God on all kinds of ground (Lk. 8:5 ff.). He is a doctor bending over the sick to care for them, for he has come to call, not the just, but sinners to repentance (Lk. 5:31–32). His mission is even clearer in the sentence: "The Son of Man has come to seek and save what is lost" (Lk. 19:10; cf. Mt. 10:6; 15:24). These texts point out that the son's "coming" and his zeal for seeking out those who had strayed (Mt. 8:12) and were lost (Lk. 15:4, 6, 8, 24, 32) were due to the divine initiative. Jesus' entire mission was directed by the will of the Father, who cannot consent to lose the least of his children (Mt. 18:13). Moved always by his Father's desires, Jesus

## Agape in the Synoptic Gospels

loved with the Father's love. Charity was the fundamental inspiration of his existence and the great motive of even his smallest acts.

How did the well-beloved son accomplish his work of love? Not by reigning in power over the people of God as a glorious Messias, but by taking our illnesses upon himself and bearing our infirmities (Mt. 8:17). He refused every attempt to make him king (Jn. 6:15) and appeared as a slave come to serve and to give up his life (Mt. 20:28; Mk. 10:45; Lk. 22:27). Although he taught with authority, not basing his doctrine on the teaching of the schools but vigorously promulgating the word of God, there was nothing in him of the haughty and demanding master. He spoke to the weary and the overburdened, inviting them gently and humbly to receive his doctrine; he promised them happiness (Mt. 5:3 ff.). His zeal, which was consuming and austere for the worship of his Father (Mt. 21:12–16), was completely patient and sensitive in dealing with men. He personified the beatitude of the peacemakers and the gentle of spirit (Mt. 5:4). Even at his triumphal entry into Jerusalem, he made no change in his extreme modesty. He exercised perfect discretion, clear-sighted tact, and a radiant kindness. The traits of the beloved outlined by his Father were plain in him: "He will not wrangle or rend the air. . . . The reed that is bruised he will not crush or quench the smoldering wick" (Mt. 12:18–21).

People called him "Good Master" (Mk. 10:17; Lk. 18:18; cf. Mt. 20:15); his loving heart was in full view of all. When he met someone faithful to his Father's will, he spontaneously loved him (Mk. 10:21). He was obviously happy with publicans and sinners, whose company he seemed to seek out (for instance, when he invited himself to visit Zacchaeus—Mt. 11:19; Lk. 7:34; cf. 10:27–32, 19:1–10; Mk. 2:13–17). Simon the leper and Martha and Mary were among his intimates (Mt. 26:6–14; Mk. 14:3–9; Lk. 10:38–42), but he cherished the Twelve in a special way and called them his friends (Lk. 12:4). Among these, Peter, James, and John seem to have held a privileged place (Mk. 5:37; Lk. 8:51—Mt. 17:1; Mk. 9:2; Lk. 9:28—22:8—Mt. 26:37; Mk. 14:33). He loved his own country, Nazareth and Jerusalem. The multiple nuances and hierarchies in his affections reveal a profound and active charity displaying itself in a thousand kindnesses. One might say that the Lord divided his days between preaching and curing the sick. From the first he gave a double sign of the authenticity of his mission by announcing the good news to the poor and by performing countless miracles for the afflicted (Lk. 4:16–22, 7:18–23). A tree is known by its fruits, and men, when they saw the divine *agape* of Christ shining in his works,[1] recognized that the kingdom of God was come.

Such was Christ, authorized witness of the Father's love. God asked men to trust his son, who had come to inaugurate the kingdom on earth, and to listen to him. The kingdom has its own morality—response to the divine initiative (1 Jn. 4:19), a welcoming of God's gift. Man is a sinner whose debt God had freely discharged, a sinner who feels the love, confidence, fidelity, and adoration that the synoptic writers sum up in the word *agape*. This is the second revelation of the Gospels. The God of Jesus Christ desires to unite himself to men

---

[1] "There is nothing hidden but must be made known some day" (Mk. 4:22).

through their response of love. Their worship and service will be made through manifestations of charity.

Thanks to the question of the doctor of the Law: "Which is the greatest commandment in the Law?" (Mt. 22:34 ff.; Mk. 12:28 ff.) the first article basic to the new morality has been defined as clearly as can be desired. According to Luke 10:25 ff., the lawyer had asked, "What must I do to inherit eternal life?" This fortunate difference in formulation of what is really one and the same question reveals that the observance of the greatest commandment is the assured means of entering eternal life and of being saved. Jesus reaffirmed the primacy of love of God that had been demanded of the chosen people from the beginning: "Love the Lord your God. . . ."

Deuteronomy demanded total consecration of heart, soul, intelligence, and strength. To love God with charity was to belong to him exclusively and without reserve. Our Lord insisted that God has a right to this homage and gift because he is the *Kyrios*, the sovereign who may ask everything because he has given everything. Man, debtor as creature even before his doubly indebting repurchase, must acknowledge him as sole master. God's supreme sovereignty makes of Christ's disciples slaves bound irrevocably to their Lord: "A man cannot be the slave of two masters. He will either hate the one and love the other, or, at least, be attentive to the one and neglectful of the other" (Mt. 6:24; Lk. 16:13). Charity is exclusive. A debtor saved from slavery ought to consecrate his restored liberty to the service of his only Lord. The disciple's consecration will demonstrate the seriousness of his religious spirit, for the most beautiful

## Agape in the New Testament

homage he can offer God is his radical attachment. The Pharisees never understood the supreme value of this attachment. They were materially exact in observing rubrics and in paying the most insignificant tithes, but they were attached primarily to the good opinion of others. They were their own great love, and they had no feeling for *agape*, the exclusive gift of the whole heart to God (Lk. 11:42). Jesus made it absolutely clear that authentic charity is both choice and renouncement; to choose is to sacrifice. Love of God outweighs all other attachments and, if necessary, dissolves them.[2] One cannot pretend to be a disciple of Christ without despising and rejecting everything that would impede fidelity to God. "He who cares more for father or mother than for me is not worthy of me; he who cares more for son or daughter than for me is not worthy of me. By gaining his life a man will lose it; by losing his life for my sake, he will gain it" (Mt. 10:37; Lk. 14:26). Human affections have to be sacrificed and natural bonds broken; suffering must be accepted. Our Lord spoke of taking up one's cross. (Lk. 9:23). Jesus came, out of love, to give his life as a ransom for many; the *agape* of his disciple reaches even to daily crucifixion. All-consuming love of God and of Christ deals death to self and the world. To set aside some part of love and life for private use, like a Pharisee hugging his little hoard, would be to corrupt the total gift which *agape* demands and to endanger eternal life (Lk. 9:24–26).

Charity is a devouring flame (Mt. 24:12) whose leaping strength and sweeping force consume everything in its path. This fire burns a way to the kingdom of heaven,

[2] Cf. the parables of the hidden treasure and the pearl (Mt. 13:44–46; cf. 18:8–9, 19:27, 29).

## Agape in the Synoptic Gospels

a kingdom proclaimed for all but demanding struggle and war for its winning (Lk. 13:24): "The kingdom of heaven is *to be taken by storm* and only by storm do men lay hold of it!" (Mt. 11:12; cf. Lk. 16:6). The verb in Greek suggests the energy indispensable for responding to God's call and forcing a way through to him. The kingdom can be taken only by assault, and only the strong can do violence to themselves and win it. Christ offered his kingdom to sinners, but how can they enter it without total conversion and costly renouncements? Their ardent gratitude (Lk. 7:42, 47) at love's initiative impels them to repent and to long for the yoke of the Gospel. Their intense zeal forces the gates of the kingdom. One of the great surprises of the Gospel is to see the "wicked," far from the ways of justice, precede the just, far from the sense of God's free gift and the courage to renounce themselves completely. "I tell you frankly: the tax collectors and the prostitutes are entering the kingdom of God ahead of you; for although John's mission was strictly within the limits of the law, you did not believe him; but the tax collectors and the prostitutes did believe him. You saw what happened, but in the end you did not feel remorse and believe him" (Mt. 21:31–32).

The third revelation of the Gospel is the demand for total sacrifice, the conceiving of Christian life as a carrying of the cross. The disciple's life is not a study in equilibrium with a nice structure of virtues all poised and counterpoised on the base of sweet reason. The disciple is a man completely emptied, his love poured out to God.

The rich young man asked the same question as the Scribe: what to do to obtain eternal life. Only one thing was lacking in his very real virtue—detachment from

## Agape in the New Testament

riches. The Lord invited him to sell what he possessed and to receive a treasure in heaven. When he refused, Jesus declared to his disciples: "How hard it is for the wealthy to enter the kingdom of God! . . . I tell you, no one gives up home, or parents, or brothers, or wife, or children, for the sake of the kingdom of God, but receives many times as much in this world and eternal life in the world to come" (Lk. 18:24–30). In one instance eternal life is promised for charity toward God and, in the other, for poverty. The sinful woman's love for the Lord made her forget all human respect and disavow her disordered life; her adoration, source of her attachment and fidelity to him, won pardon for her sins (Lk. 7:47). In all three instances, it was the Lord's initiative of love that brought about renouncement of self, contempt for the world, and liberation from created goods. Men are amazed, as was the young man at his first encounter with Christian morality, to find it so strict. It is strict because it is a religious morality. The primacy of the love of God (*agape tou theou*) rules not only conduct but also thoughts and affections. Religious consecration must be total; love of God has to be exclusive. Christian morality is essentially interior (Mt. 23:24–28; cf. 18:35; Lk. 10:27).

The Gospel gives a fourth major revelation: the importance of love of neighbor. It seems to tell us that our behavior toward others should be summed up in *agape*. According to St. Luke, the charter of the kingdom, promulgated in the Sermon on the Mount, consists in a single precept with endless applications: Love! (Lk. 6:27). That is why the second commandment is assimilated to the first in such a basic way, until the one word, *agape*,

## Agape in the Synoptic Gospels

describes both loves. When our Lord was asked what to do to obtain eternal life or what was the greatest commandment, he could only prescribe the love of God, but he added that love of neighbor was a similar commandment, of the same order and importance. All Christian morality depends upon these two precepts (Mt. 22: 34-40; Mk. 7: 17-23, 12:28-34; Lk. 10:25-37). Nothing will have significance for God, nothing will be religiously correct or good unless it is inspired and carried out by authentic charity. It would be impossible to say more clearly that Christian morality is a morality of love. Christ's disciple is a man who loves.

It is perhaps surprising to realize that the duty of loving one's neighbor seems to prevail over duty toward God. Fraternal love is more important than holocausts or sacrifices (Mk. 12:33). It is indispensable to the acceptance of our gift that, before offering it, we make peace with anyone who has a grievance against us: "If you are about to offer your gift at the altar, and there remember that your brother holds something against you, leave your gift there before the altar, and first go and settle your argument with your brother; and then come back and offer your gift" (Mt. 5:23-24). It would seem that Christians will be declared just and invited into eternal life at the Last Judgment in proportion to their mercy and kindness to the poor (Mt. 22:40). The Lord will consider every kindness done to these humble persons he calls his brothers as addressed to himself (Mt. 25:40). Not only will Christians love their neighbor because their love for God leads them to do what he commands —their conduct would have no religious value unless it proceeded from this love—but also because they see

## Agape in the New Testament

Christ, their unique beloved, in their brothers: "You did it to me!"

*Agape* is an active and effective love operating with a singular tenderness. The Sermon on the Mount stressed its heroic forms of patience and of gentleness. The parable of the Good Samaritan shows it to be attentive and tender, truly compassionate. *Agape* will be able to minister openly and unreservedly to a neighbor, but only from an utterly selfless heart. It would never occur to someone who clings to his comfort, peace, honor, or possessions to care for an injured person or to give his food and clothing away. He would never consent to give up his tunic, proffer his cheek to blows, or pardon without limit (Mt. 18:21–35), even when yielding to "indiscreet" requests might have allowed peace to triumph at last and gentleness to prevail over violence and injustice. Love of neighbor requires as total a renouncement as does love of God. In the Gospel, to love means to give, to give oneself, to belong to another—to belong to God in obedience and consecration, to belong to neighbor in service and compassion. In either case autonomy and liberty are put aside for the sake of the beloved. The sacrifices, the stripping away, and the death to self accomplished by charity are made easier by the certainty of reward: the hundredfold of joy and spiritual goods in this life and the treasure of eternal life in heaven (Mt. 19:19; Lk. 10:28). *Agape* is worship far surpassing burnt offerings and sacrifices (Mk. 12:33). Holocausts used to lead to forgiveness of sin; now *agape* assures us of pardon (Lk. 7:47). "Go and learn what is meant by the words, 'Compassion is what I desire, and not sacrifice'" (Mt. 9:13; cf. 12:7).

## Agape in the Synoptic Gospels

At this point we can understand how and why the Lord, bringing the Old Law to its highest point of perfection, could present a man's enemies as the privileged object of his charity (Mt. 5:43–48; Lk. 6:27–36). No other object would call for such forgetfulness of self, such absence of egoism. To will good to enemies, to pray for them, and to serve them is an act of perfectly free generosity because it in no way depends on any lovableness in its object. In demanding love of enemies, Jesus radically distinguished love of charity from love of friendship. Friendship is founded on mutual liking; it springs from the appreciation of another's qualities and gifts (Lk. 7:5). It is by nature reciprocal. Charity is neither passion nor ordinary liking. It is a pure and spiritual desire for the good, rooted deep in the heart. The charitable man loves those who are spiteful and unresponsive. He does good to those who do evil to him. Spiritual love is its own motive. Just as light by nature illuminates, so also fire warms, and charity manifests goodness in overflowing generosity. There is no point in looking for the reason of a nature. We can see, then, why Jesus never asked his disciples to love all men in their humanity. His "social morality" was no philanthropy built upon a humanitarian conception of the brotherhood of all men united by their common nature, by their human dignity, and by the divine spark of intelligence and will each possessed. Jesus chose "neighbors" of such evident wickedness for his concrete examples that it would have been nonsense to command them to be loved out of friendship or philanthropy.

Nevertheless, these "neighbors" are to be loved with

## Agape in the New Testament

charity because God loves them. They are to be loved in the way he loves them. This is the Gospel's fifth revelation. God lavishes his gifts on sinners and on the ungrateful, without expecting any return. Christians, who are his sons, must resemble their Father in thought, in heart, and in conduct. The reason for the disciple's *agape* is his divine sonship (Lk. 6:35), which necessarily brings participation and resemblance with it. Many other virtues might have been singled out as the criterion for sonship between the faithful and their Father in heaven; the Lord chose love. In the final analysis, the morality of the Gospel rests on the principle that we are to be perfect as the heavenly Father is perfect (Mt. 5:48), and merciful as he is merciful (Lk. 6:36). This means not just loving, but loving perfectly, loving divinely, according to his example and to his command. To love as God loves is to love with the same breadth in objects, the same ingenuity in activity, the same purity in intention. To love with God's love is the goal of love; in the light of this goal, simply human love changes in nature and is transmuted into *agape*. It gradually takes on a divine mode of behavior. Although no one can be assimilated entirely to this divine mode here on earth, everyone can discover its essential qualities of gratuitousness, generosity, and universality, and everyone must tend unceasingly to approach it as an ideal. Some love less, others more; there are degrees in love of neighbor as there are in love of God (Lk. 7:42, 47). Here, too, great sinners rejoicing in pardon will be spontaneously inclined to be merciful and generous toward their brothers. Having a deeper experience of the gratuitousness of God's gift, they feel obliged to show themselves "better," to give to other men as God has given to them (Mt. 18:21–35; cf. 5:7, 6:14, 7:1; Lk. 11:4).

The first man tried to become "like God" (Gn. 3:5). By the charity which makes him die to himself, the disciple of Jesus in God's kingdom on earth can be truly transformed and transfigured into God. The resemblance will be so visible and exact that no one can mistake it. His good works will glow like light from a lamp. His charity is avid to prove itself, for it is the very love of God which must be revealed to the world. It will burn with such brilliance that men will discover and acclaim God's own goodness in its "works." Giving praise was constantly revealed as the natural result of the Lord's mercy and wonderful kindness (Mt. 9:8, 15:31; Lk. 7:16, 13:13, 17:15, 18:43, 23:47). It belongs to the disciple to continue the revelation of God's goodness by his charity, to bring all men of good will to echo his praises.

Having discovered the constituent parts of *agape*, it is possible to define the love of charity as it was understood by the first disciples of Jesus. The notion is extremely complex. The Evangelists use only one word in describing many kinds of attachments—the love of the Father for his only son, the compassion of the Good Samaritan, the centurion's respect and veneration for the Jewish nation, the Pharisees' yearnings to be first, and the virtue par excellence of Jesus' disciples. Only the religious meanings are pertinent here.

In God, the model of *agape*, charity appears as the most noble of loves, a sovereign respect and delight in

## Agape in the New Testament

Christ and a desire for good to men. Its characteristics are gratuitousness, disinterestedness, and generosity. God's charity takes the initiative in granting pardon and salvation, pouring out its kindnesses, and revealing itself in active mercy. In the Christian, *agape* is primarily an adoration of God that is marked by consecration, by fidelity, and also—to judge from the sinful woman—by respectful tenderness and lively emotion. With regard to neighbor, this love requires the same total gift as the love of God. It implies real service and unlimited, untiring kindness. The parable of the Good Samaritan shows charity's possible identification with mercy as spontaneous compassion and human emotion. The Greeks understood esteem or veneration when they used the word *agape*, but *agape* in the Gospels is much more than that. It is more even than heroic devotion. It is love properly so-called, the fundamental goodness of heart. Accordingly, its characteristics most stressed in the synoptic Gospels are patience, gentleness, and meekness. Christ's whole life was a manifestation of *agape*. Only he could have united in such harmony exquisite benignity and the total gift of self, even to the sacrifice of his life. His complete consecration to his Father's will commanded a life of humble service to men. In the same way, Christians will be able to love neighbor only when they are entirely given to the service of God. Love of God (*agape tou theou*) is the source of fraternal charity and of the whole Gospel morality.

In the synoptic Gospels, then, *agape* is essentially a deep-rooted, conscious love, seeking always to prove itself. It is God's free gift received by man and returned to him with deep gratitude. Toward neighbor it is spon-

## Agape in the Synoptic Gospels

taneous, disinterested, and gentle. It forces men to decision and moves them to act to translate their love into kindnesses or into services (Mt. 5:42). *Agape* implies being unconditionally available; it may demand the sacrifice of all that is humanly dear.

# List of Texts Analyzed

Mt. 3:17
Mt. 5:43–48
Mt. 6:24
Mt. 12:18
Mt. 17:5
Mt. 19:19
Mt. 22:37, 39
Mt. 24:12

Mk. 1:11
Mk. 9:7
Mk. 10:21

Mk. 12:6
Mk. 12:30–33

Lk. 3:22
Lk. 6:27, 32, 35
Lk. 7:5
Lk. 7:42–47
Lk. 10:27
Lk. 11:42
Lk. 11:43
Lk. 16:13
Lk. 20:13

# Index

Accusations, 34
Admiration, Christ's, 62
Adoration, 17, 56, 63, 73, 102, 104, 107, 142
*Agape,*
   active love, 138
   benevolence, 40, 84, 100
   choice, 16 ff., 62, 134
   cult, 66
   degrees, 54, 106, 123, 140
   delight, 39-40, 43, 47
   disinterested, 84-85, 115
   esteem, 18, 62, 92
   exclusive attachment, 18, 64
   expiates sin, 102-3, 130
   generosity, 72, 85
   gratuitous, 85-87
   kindliness, 12, 52
   influence over the virtues, 25, 64
   loss, 54
   manifest, 94, 101, 119, 143
   object, 29, 52
   permanent, 18, 104
   plenitude, 54
   prayer, 52, 53
   preference, 17, 122
   reciprocal, 85-86
   religious consecration, 51, 65, 105
   respect, 97, 102, 122
   response of gratitude, 64, 100-101, 103, 106
   spontaneous, 115
   tenderness, 72, 124, 138, 142
   *See also* Love, Charity, Mercy
Agreement of wills, 40
Alms, 25
Anger of God, 71
Anointing with perfume, 97

*Index*

Apostasy, 33
Applause, love of, 118

Baptism of Jesus, 37 ff.
Benignity, 61
  of God, 13
Brother of Jesus, 137

Calvary,
  *See* Cross
Caress, 60
Centurion, 92
Charism, 38
Charity,
  definition, 141 ff.
  divine sonship, 13, 140
  extension, 14
  generous, 82-84, 88, 134, 138
  love properly so-called, 142
  motive of, 12, 52
  sacrifice, 81
  sons of God, 89
  steadfast virtue, 83
  toward God, 120-22
Chiton, 81
Christian,
  a son of God, 12 ff.
Church, 71
Cloud, 42
Commandments, the greatest, 62 ff., 133
  reduction to unity, 31
  the second, 136-37
  weighty, 121
Compassion, 116, 138
Consecration to God, 133, 135-36, 138
Constraint,
  bodily, 99
Content,
  to be, 119
Conversion, 130
Covenant,
  new and old, 5 ff., 62 ff., 77 ff., 111

*Index*

Creditor, 99-100
Cross,
    to carry one's, 134-36
Curses against the Pharisees, 120

Death,
  *See* Cross
Debt and sin, 130
Debtor, 99-101, 133
Desire and charity, 102, 118-19
Disciple, beloved of God, 129
    exclusive, 133-35
    loving, 77-78, 124, 136-37
    virtuous, 136-38
Discretion of Jesus, 46
Disdain, 18
Disposition, interior, 32
Doctors of lies, 33-34

Elect, the, 46 ff.
Enemy, 8 ff., 79-80, 139-40
Esteem, 18, 92
Evil, the height of, 34-35
Example, 110
    concrete, 139
    *See also* Imitation

Faith and charity, 73, 107
Fidelity, 18-19, 25
    and charity, 35, 36, 40, 51, 55, 63, 123
Fire and charity, 36, 54, 134
Friend and enemy, 85-86

Gaze of Jesus, 60 ff.
Gentiles, 71
Glory,
   light of, 41-42
   power, 44
God,
   compassionate, 89, 124-25
   Father, 7, 14
   his creatures, 115

*Index*

**God** (*continued*)
  his rights, 133-34
  kind and generous, 88, 129
  longsuffering, 68
  lovable, 73
  loves his son, 45, 46-49, 49 ff., 67 ff.
  loving, 13, 72, 140
  model of charity, 141
  new conception, 7
  retribution, 86, 91
  *See also* Paternity
Good, the, 20, 139, 142
Gospel, the,
  according to the Hebrews, 23
  summed up in charity, 79
  in mercy, 106
Growing cold of charity, 32 ff.

Hatred, 33-34, 48, 55
  on the part of the world, 79-80
Heir (Christ), 69
Heresy, 34
Himation, 81
Holy Spirit and Jesus, 38-39
Homage and love, 102
Hospitality, 61

Imitation of God, 12 ff., 26, 29, 89, 124-25, 140
Iniquity, 32-35

James, 46
Jesus,
  a doctor, 130
  and charity, 131-32
  and his Father, 39, 43, 129-30
  and the Torah, 27
  a prophet, 99
  his charity, 96 ff.
  his compassion, 115-16, 123
  his discretion, 46
  his divinity, 107
  his kindness, 61-62, 142-43

## Index

Jesus (*continued*)
  his love of men, 48-49
  his meekness, 48
  the Son of God, 37, 45, 49-50, 68-69
John, 46
Joy, 61
  eschatological, 91–92
  spiritual, 88
Judge, to, 90
Judgment of God, 137
Just, the, 135, 137
Justice,
  legal, 6-7
  moral, 121-22
  of the disciples, 5 ff., 15

Kiss, 61
  a mark of submission, 98
Kingdom of God, 130
  taken by storm, 135

Law, 6-7
  and religious life, 27, 29, 51-52
Lawyer, 26
Legalism, 6-7
Letter,
  obedience of the, 7
Liberty and charity, 51-54, 139
Life, eternal, 19
  and fraternal charity, 22-23, 110 ff.
  and renouncement, 135-36
  and vocation, 62
Loan, 86
Longsuffering,
  God's, 67-71
Love, and hate, 9, 84, 133
  extension, 114-15
  for God *and* neighbor, 8 ff., 26 ff., 52-54, 64 ff., 91, 122-25, 136-37
  for other men, 52-53
  innovation, 78-79
  kindness, 80, 85
  man's love for God, 51

## Index

Love (*continued*)
   the mark of Christ's disciples, 73-78, 124
   the supreme commandment, 73

Meek,
   beatitude of the, 131-32, 137-38, 142
Meekness, 48-49, 67-68
Mercy and charity, 85, 88-90, 116 ff., 121, 124-25, 130, 138
Messias,
   his character, 46 ff., 50-51
Morality, new, 15, 20, 123-24, 133
   demanding, 135-36
   filial, 91, 139-40
   interior, 7 ff., 32, 66
   its foundation and inspiration, 26, 29 ff., 55-56, 62 ff.
   obedient, 25
   religious, 140-41
Moses, 45
Mystery of iniquity, 32 ff.

Neighbor, 10 ff., 65, 136 ff.
   to act as a, 108 ff.

Obedience,
   to God, 74
   to the law, 60

Pagan,
   *See* Gentiles
Pardon,
   of God, 102-6
   to one's neighbor, 89-90
Parousia,
   its prelude, 33
Passion of Jesus foretold, 43-46, 67-71
Paternity of God, 53, 129, 140
Patience, 138-40
Perfection of the disciples by *agape*, 13-14, 18, 53-54, 124
   interior, 16
   presupposes poverty, 22 ff., 52-53
   proposed, not imposed, 81-82
Persecution and happiness, 32 ff.

## Index

Perseverance of love, 50, 54-55
   condition of salvation, 36
Peter, 46
Pharisee, 46, 48, 118, 120
Philanthropy, 139
Pity, 124-25
Praise of God, 141
Prayer for enemies, 11-12
Precedence, 118
Predilection,
   divine, 72-73
   of Christ, 62, 73
   of Christians, 133-34
Prophet, 67
Providence, 68-69, 72-73
Publican, 12, 135

Reciprocity toward God, 132-33
   *See also* Agape
Recompense, 85-86, 87, 91, 125
Remission of sins,
   and love, 102-4, 105
Renouncement, 81-83, 87, 135 ff., 138
Resemblance, 28
Reverence and charity, 97-98
Rich young man, 59 ff.
Riches, 16 ff., 21 ff.
   and perfection, 60-61, 135-36
Rule,
   golden, 83

Sacrifice of self, 81
   total, 135-36
   *See also* Cross
Samaritan, 113 ff.
   the good, 108 ff.
Scandal, 33-35, 54-55
Scribe, 63, 118
Sermon on the Mount, 5 ff., 52-53, 77 ff., **122-23**
Servant of Yahweh, 46-47
Service of God and charity, 16 ff.
Shekinah, 42

## Index

Sinner, 130, 132, 135
Slave, 16-17, 67
   before God, 133-34
   in the pagan world, 92-93
Smile of Christ, 61
Son of God, 88, 91, 114, 124
   resembles his Father, 140
Synagogue, 118

Tenderness,
   for one's neighbor, 114-16
   of Christ, 117
Theology, biblical, vi
Tithes, 120
Transfiguration, 41
Treasure, 16, 24-25
Tribulation, 32 ff.

Veneration, 101-2, 105
Vinedressers,
   the murderous, 67 ff.
Violence,
   salutary, 135
Voice from heaven, 37 ff., 42 ff.

Wages, 99-100
Wickedness of men, 68
Woman,
   the sinful, 95 ff.
Works,
   good, 17, 20, 140
Worship, 138

www.ingramcontent.com/pod-product-compliance
Lightning Source LLC
Chambersburg PA
CBHW051938160426
43198CB00013B/2200